AGRICULTURAL PRODUCTS
AND MARKETS

OECD FOOD INDUSTRIES IN THE 1980s

ORGANISATION FOR ECONOMIC CO-OPERATION AND DEVELOPMENT

Pursuant to article 1 of the Convention signed in Paris on 14th December, 1960, and which came into force on 30th September, 1961, the Organisation for Economic Co-operation and Development (OECD) shall promote policies designed:

- to achieve the highest sustainable economic growth and employment and a rising standard of living in Member countries, while maintaining financial stability, and thus to contribute to the development of the world economy;
- to contribute to sound economic expansion in Member as well as non-member countries in the process of economic development; and
- to contribute to the expansion of world trade on a multilateral, non-discriminatory basis in accordance with international obligations.

The Signatories of the Convention on the OECD are Austria, Belgium, Canada, Denmark, France, the Federal Republic of Germany, Greece, Iceland, Ireland, Italy, Luxembourg, the Netherlands, Norway, Portugal, Spain, Sweden, Switzerland, Turkey, the United Kingdom and the United States. The following countries acceded subsequently to this Convention (the dates are those on which the instruments of accession were deposited): Japan (28th April, 1964), Finland (28th January, 1969), Australia (7th June, 1971) and New Zealand (29th May, 1973).

The Socialist Federal Republic of Yugoslavia takes part in certain work of the OECD (agreement of 28th October, 1961).

Publié en français sous le titre:

LES INDUSTRIES ALIMENTAIRES DE L'OCDE
DANS LES ANNÉES 80

The programme of the Committee for Agriculture included during the last ten years activities designed to improve the structure and efficiency of food systems. The implementation of these activities has been the particular responsibility of the Ad Hoc Group on "Agro-Food Chains".

As part of its activities, this Committee, in collaboration with the Technical Co-operation Committee, organised a symposium on "The Adjustment and the Challenges Facing the Food Industries in the 1980s" in January, 1982, at OECD Headquarters.

This symposium was attended by more than 80 experts from 18 Member countries and 10 international governmental and non-governmental organisations. The participants came from Governmental Services, Universities, Research Institutes, Corporate Firms, Trade Associations and Consumer Organisations. Four major themes have been discussed:

(Theme I)
Structural Adjustment in the Food Industries. Discussions chaired by F. Lepatre, Chairman, Confédération des Industries Agro-Alimentaires de la Communauté Européenne

(Theme II)
Changes in the Relations between Food Processing and Agricultural Production, Food Distribution and Consumption. Discussions chaired by P. Sørensen, Managing Director, Nestlé Nordisk A/S

(Theme III)
Managing the development of Agro-Food Industries in Rural Areas. Discussions chaired by J.M. Rodriguez-Molina, Director General, Directorate for Food Industries, Ministry of Agriculture of Spain.

(Theme IV)
Outlook for the Food Industries and Related Government Policies in the Eighties. Discussions chaired by G. Viatte, Deputy Director, Directorate for Food, Agriculture and Fisheries, (OCDE).

The present report, based on that Symposium, includes an overall synthesis prepared by the OECD Secretariat and the Ad Hoc Group. This report was approved by the Committee for Agriculture in April, 1983, and was derestricted by the OECD Council on June 10th, 1983.

Also available

PRICE FORMATION AND THE PERFORMANCE OF AGRO-FOOD SYSTEMS (December 1982)
(51 82 07 1) ISBN 92-64-12388-1 36 pages £3.30 US$6.50 F33.00

POSITIVE ADJUSTMENT POLICIES IN THE DAIRY SECTOR (October 1983)
(51 83 09 1) ISBN 92-64-12515-9 120 pages £5.50 US$11.00 F55.00

REVIEW OF AGRICULTURAL POLICIES IN OECD MEMBER COUNTRIES 1980-1982 (October 1983)
(51 83 07 1) ISBN 92-64-12504-3 218 pages £7.50 US$15.00 F75.00

TABLE OF CONTENTS

Part I

MAIN ISSUES FACING THE FOOD INDUSTRIES

Part II

CONSOLIDATED REPORTS PRESENTED BY THE OECD CONSULTANTS FOR THE FOUR THEMES OF THE SYMPOSIUM

Part III

SHORT SUMMARIES OF THE CONTRIBUTIONS PRESENTED AT THE SYMPOSIUM

NOTE

The full text of the contributions may be obtained, free of charge, on request to the OECD Directorate for Food, Agriculture and Fisheries, for as long as stocks are available.

Part I

MAIN ISSUES FACING THE FOOD INDUSTRIES

A. THE SOCIO-ECONOMIC ENVIRONMENT FACING THE FOOD INDUSTRIES IN THE 1980s(1)

The food industries in the 1980s face the prospect of an uncertain economic environment, partly because of the differences which exist between OECD countries and partly because of the problems of forecasting future economic developments. Nevertheless, it is reasonable to expect that some of the more disquieting recent tendencies will continue into the medium term viz. slow economic growth, persistent inflation, continued disequilibria in the balance of payments of some countries, high real interest rates and slow growth in real incomes. Historically high rates of unemployment seem likely to persist, due to structural factors, notably the rigidity of labour and product markets, changes in international competitiveness, the effect of the tax structure upon employment and investment, and the impact of continued change in technology and consumer preferences.

Another important group of factors which may influence the food industries lie somewhere between the economic and the social. The decade will be marked by a mounting concern for a new "quality of life", changing attitudes towards work and leisure and increasing concern with health and environmental considerations.

Together with these general socio-economic conditions which will influence the business environment, the dynamics of the agro-food sector itself will have a decisive impact on enterprises in the sector. Significant factors here include:

- slow growth in demand for food products and continued changes in the pattern of that demand;
- higher costs due to the production of more highly processed foods;
- the need for constant innovation in a competitive business environment;
- the need to incorporate new technologies, especially developments in biotechnology;

---

1. National differences exist in the OECD area in the definition of those industries which constitute the food industry sector. In the present study, it is assumed that "Food Industries" includes the major groups of 311, 312 and 313 of the International Standard Industrial Classification ISIC (see Annex 1).

- greater interest and pressures from producers and consumers in the political arena;
- pressure from the large-scale distributors, whose market power has now become formidable;
- greater competition in the international market concurrent with increasing protectionist tendencies on the part of governments in both OECD and non-OECD countries.

During recent decades, the share of food in private consumption expenditure has been declining in most countries, though at different rates. The decline has slowed down in those countries with the highest incomes per head. In real terms, expenditure on food has continued to rise in almost all OECD Member countries(2). This has been due to continuing population growth in most countries, and an increase in expenditure per head as consumers purchase more prepared or high-quality foods and consume more foods prepared outside the home. With the slow increase in consumer earnings, which will doubtless be the case in most countries, total demand for food products and real expenditure will probably increase more slowly in the 1980s than in the 1970s, although rates will vary across countries.

The trend in demand depends not only on food prices and incomes but on many other factors (lifestlye, nutrition, physiology etc.). There will consequently be instances of "saturation" and caloric intake will stabilize or increase only slightly in the richest countries, however in these countries the consumption pattern will change. Demand will be influenced in the future by socio-demographic factors, such as the aging of the population and the growing number of women working outside the home. These factors will probably increase the demand for foods for the elderly and for prepared foods. Many countries are experiencing increasing demand for "natural" or "diet" products and for food consumed outside the home.

In most OECD countries, during the post-war period of economic growth, the cost of processing and distribution of food products has tended to absorb an increasing share of consumer food expenditure. The average for the sector as a whole is currently about 50 per cent in the most advanced countries, with a range of 15 to 85 per cent depending on the particular agricultural product. However, recent data show that this share has latterly been tending to stabilize in the United States and Germany.

The level of industry profit margins, which are becoming more difficult to measure as increasingly

---

2. However, during the period 1977-1980 food consumption in real terms fell back slightly in Canada (by 0.7 per cent annually) and Switzerland (0.1 per cent annually).

sophisticated products proliferate, is of concern to enterprises and government(3). Margins are sensitive to higher energy, manpower and financing costs. Pressures on profits will probably encourage processors to try to obtain a higher percentage of the final price for their products. Similarly, consumer concern about food costs at a time of slowly rising incomes will probably increase during the years ahead. This may be reflected by greater sensitivity to price for some products. Consumer pressures will doubtless be exercised in the matter of taxes which affect consumer prices, and other matters such as labelling and product information, quality and other aspects of "consumer protection".

The development of biotechnology will probably exert an influence on the environment of the processing industries in the 1980s, and could affect the sources or nature of raw material supply for the food industries, their production processes and even the kinds of product they market. Wider choice of raw materials could have important consequences for agricultural production(4).

The changing socio-economic environment is creating a set of external constraints which enterprises will have to take account of in their day-to-day management and in their medium and long-term development strategies.

B. STRUCTURAL ADJUSTMENTS IN THE FOOD INDUSTRIES(5)

In the OECD countries, the food industry share of Gross Domestic Product (measured by value added) ranged from 2.3 per cent in the United States to more than 5 per cent in Ireland and New Zealand in 1980. The relative prominence of the sector has tended to decline since the value of its output has grown more slowly than total GDP.

The relatively slow growth of demand for food products has contributed to the vigorous competition in the food industry and prompted rapid structural change. This

---

3. For a more detailed analysis, see OECD "Food Margins Analysis: Aims, Methods and Uses". Paris 1981.

4. Major developments in biotechnology have been reviewed in OECD "Biotechnology: International Trends and Prospects", Paris 1982.

5. Data availability and comparability present considerable problems in deriving international comparisons. Due to the size of the task, no attempt has been made in this report to provide a comprehensive and comparable set of statistics on the food industries in OECD Member countries. The existence of such statistics would provide a major aid to analysis of food industry issues.

has varied across countries and branches of the industry, making generalisation difficult.

There is increasing differentiation in the agricultural product processing industries between primary and secondary processors. The latter essentially produce foodstuffs for the consumer from semi-finished products supplied by the primary processing industries.

Enterprises in the primary processing industry produce either simple, comparatively homogeneous or undifferentiated products like sugar and flour, which may be sold directly to the consumer but are also used by secondary processing industries, or ingredients such as gluten, starch and lactose (through what amounts to biochemical "cracking") for use by other food and non-food processing industries. The primary industries process heavy agricultural raw materials and are usually located close to production areas or for imported materials close to ports. Their main objectives are to have access to reliable and stable sources of supply, to maximise the utilisation of by-products and to maintain product quality.

Secondary processing enterprises produce branded products with increasingly sophisticated and diversified presentation and packaging. Their main objective is to differentiate their products from those of competitors. They practise all the techniques of non-price competition in marketing, e.g. advertising and sales promotion.

The primary processing sector is still closely linked to agriculture, whereas the secondary sector is becoming increasingly similar in structure to other branches of the manufacturing sector.

Structural adjustment is a complicated and multifaceted process. It is determined simultaneously by trends and fluctuations in supply and demand and by the feedback effects of enterprise behaviour and performance. Analysis of these adjustments over the long term is still at an early stage.

Although there are problems of data availability and comparability, concentration of the food processing industry seems to be marked in most OECD countries. Concentration has intensified over the last two or three decades and is average or above average in relation to other major manufacturing groups. Concentration is highest in the wheat, coffee, chocolate, soluble powders, wine, beer and spirits industries with a few exceptions (e.g. beer and wine in Germany). It is also high for consumer-ready products such as canned soups, baby foods, frozen meals, breakfast cereals, chocolate confectionery, canned milk, potato preparations and instant soups, ice cream and margarine. Concentration is also high for a few of the non-differentiated products, notably sugar and vegetable oil and starch products. Other industries, such as those producing milk, flour, health beverages and pet foods, are much less concentrated, though there is an increasing tendency towards this.

Some enterprises remain specialised, others still include a variety of different activities, some upstream, some downstream, and some unrelated to agriculture. The management of the enterprise, in particular their objectives and perceptions, has a strong influence upon integration or diversification.

Thus the food industry in most countries usually comprises a concentrated sector plus a sector consisting of small and medium sized enterprises. Many firms are becoming multinational in their operations, as a result of their development strategies and their adaptation to national policies.

The effects of international trade and foreign investment on the structure of the food industry are difficult to identify. There is insufficient information at present for a complete assessment of the impact of these factors on the performance of food industries in the countries concerned. Generally speaking, the development of trade seems to promote increased competition, while foreign investment is associated with high levels of concentration and product differentiation. Such investment permits economices of scale in marketing, research and development (R & D), and distribution, rather than in production. The increasing concentration and internationalisation of the food industry cannot be explained solely in terms of economies of scale and the better use of resources. It is also a reaction to governments' protectionist and taxation policies. Obstacles to international trade are one of the factors that make enterprises invest abroad in order to expand and diversify. Trade and foreign investment are apparently playing an important role in the international convergence of food industry structures.

A better understanding of structural evolution in the food industry requires the definition and analysis of concepts such as "performance" and "competition". One difficulty is that "performance" and "competition" are not seen in the same way by an enterprise and by society. In fact it is useful, especially in oligopolistic industries, to distinguish between economic rivalry (between enterprises) taking the form of non-price competition (product differentiation, advertising, etc.) and competition in the traditional sense which is limited to price competition. It is necessary to improve the statistical base and to standardize techniques for the measurement of "private" and "social" performance, and competition and productivity to be able to make useful comparisons, especially between countries.

In summary, the internationalisation of the food industry is becoming more marked, both through direct foreign investment and through the growth of trade. The outcome is a certain degree of convergence of food industry structures and operations between OECD countries. Trade with developing countries, some of which have a comparative advantage in this area is also a factor (e.g. the extension of the system of generalised preferences, less protectionism etc.) but has not been explored in depth(6).

In spite of the international convergence in structures, there is still no sign of a similar convergence at international level in other important areas such as pricing and marketing strategies and government regulations in all fields, including foreign trade. Here national differences are still apparent. An exception is provided by the European Economic Community for which there exists a customs union and the increasing harmonization of national legislation.

C. DYNAMICS OF THE RELATIONSHIPS BETWEEN FOOD INDUSTRIES AND UPSTREAM AND DOWNSTREAM ACTIVITIES

The relationships between the food industries and other elements in the food chain reflect their relative economic or political power. Following a process of concentration (noted above) the food processing industries have arrived at an oligopolistic structure for the majority of branches in most OECD countries, giving them considerable economic power. Agricultural producers are usually numerous and scattered but they remain a potent political force. They frequently group together, either to retain control over the market for their primary output (bargaining co-operatives) or to process it (processing co-operatives). Distributors are also concentrated and their bargaining power has grown considerably. While consumers are becoming increasingly well educated and informed, they are a numerous and scattered group. The greater awareness of the potential political power of the consumer has given rise to the formation of a number of consumer associations which aim to achieve various objectives. In some cases it has stimulated the growth of consumer co-operatives. Unfortunately, the relationships between the various actors in the food chain which are changing rapidly have still not been investigated sufficiently.

---

6. UNIDO arranged a conference on the food industry in November 1981 to encourage the growth of this sector in the developing countries.

The processing industries must ensure regular supplies of their raw materials. With the exception of arrangements involving processing co-operatives, most processors contract with individual producers (poultry, fruit and vegetables, textile fibres) or negotiate with producer groups, bargaining co-operatives or marketing boards. In some cases, producers form processing co-operatives and process their own products. However, the development of co-operatives has been uneven among countries and across products. Some governments provide facilities or financial incentives to the co-operative sector or to producers' groups to encourage their growth. In some countries there has been a substantial expansion in the role of co-operatives (in Sweden for example where they account for almost the entire amount of agricultural production and 50 per cent of agricultural processing). The growth of co-operatives may substantially alter the competitive conditions in the food industries and thus affect their economic performance.

In relations between the food industries and the retail trade, an essential feature has been the recent growth in the economic power of the major food distributors. This growth has affected not only the size of retail outlets but also the percentage of total food product sales for which they account. Concentration in retailing in many countries has affected the balance of economic power between processors and distributors and the competitive relationship between the two groups. Some processors have made attempts to integrate retailing into their activities but most of these have proved to be unsuccessful. There are substantial natural barriers to such integration, in particular the different management skills required by the two types of business activity. In addition, processors who have attempted such integration have sometimes encountered resistance from existing retailers or difficulties with anti-trust legislation. Similarly, differences in structure and operating characteristics provide natural barriers to the integration of processing into the activities of retailers. However, a number of retailers (e.g. Migros in Switzerland) are moving into food processing. Where retailers can obtain favourable terms for the supply of products from processors and can find opportunities for further growth in food or other branches of retailing it is unlikely that this trend will become widespread. In many countries (e.g. the United Kingdom and the United States) large retailers have generally found it easier and more profitable to develop their retailing operations outside of traditional food lines rather than to develop integrated processing and retailing activities in food.

Large-scale distribution tends to reduce the dispersion of prices for similar products and to produce a favourable price/quality ratio for the consumer. However, in some countries various problems have arisen e.g. the availability of a restricted range of consumer products and the inadequate transmission of consumer requirements with respect to product type and quality. There have however been instances of the distribution sector making an attempt to inform and to communicate better with the consumer.

Consumers, who are not generally in direct contact with the processing industries, are pressing for better consumer education, information and protection. As a result the food industries and distributors are becoming increasingly attentive to consumers. Some have developed special departments to improve consumer relations and have expanded research into consumer preferences and attitudes.

Changes in the structure of the food industries, in their relationship to other elements of the food chain, and in the form of food products themselves have all influenced the nature and degree of competition in the food industry. The greatest price competition tends to occur with respect to standardized, unsophisticated products in situations fairly close to perfect competition, i.e. where there are numerous purchasers and numerous sellers and substantial transparency of information. This situation is becoming less and less common. Where there is imperfect competition, price discrimination can be practised for the benefit of the stronger economic agents(7).

The growth of large processing firms has led to the development of branded goods which in many cases are produced and marketed multinationally. For most of these non-price competition increasingly prevails(8). It is not clear whether such competition benefits the consumer or not. In some countries, there is an increasing tendency for retailers to market products under their own brands or as unbranded (generic) goods. Most of these are manufactured by food processors under contract with distributors; these processors may be large enterprises or small or medium enterprises according to the products concerned. This development has provided for continued competition on the basis of price for basic consumer products, even as competition relating to branded varieties of these products has tended to become increasingly non-price in nature.

---

7. Food price formation is analysed in the OECD study: "Price Formation and Performance of Agro-Food Systems in OECD Countries", Paris, 1982.

8. Non-price competition is that undertaken by firms through such activities as advertising and promotion which aim to differentiate their products i.e. to establish unique attributes of the products in the minds of consumers.

The growth of large-scale distribution has not only affected competition in the food industries but has also created new modes of behaviour in retailing. Advertising, promotion and the differential pricing of similar products both through time and by location have become more widespread. Frequently, the distributor's strategies are such that systematic comparisons are hard to make, because products are priced differently from one shop to another and some are used as loss leaders, while ensuring a profitable margin on the entire range of products. As yet, consumers and public authorities have not found any effective way of preventing this. Indeed its prevention through government intervention may be undesirable since the measures typically employed (price controls, limits on the establishment of supermarkets etc.) may disrupt the functioning of market forces.

Changes in the structure of the food industries and in their relationships with other groups in the food chain have implications for their economic performance. Governments respond to these changes and in some cases may initiate or contribute to them. The role of government in relation to the food industry is therefore the focus of discussion in the remainder of this section of the report.

D. PUBLIC MANAGEMENT ISSUES RELATED TO THE AGRO-FOOD INDUSTRY IN RURAL AREAS

Over the past few decades, the progressive modernisation and mechanisation of agriculture, accompanied by an increase in average farm-size has allowed for a substantial increase in agricultural productivity. This in turn has resulted in labour migration and facilitated the development of other, predominantly urban, sectors of the economy. In the last few years, several factors, most importanly the increasing level of unemployment in OECD countries, have led to renewed interest in developing the economy of rural areas and in fully utilising their local resources. While agriculture remains the dominant economic activity in such areas, considerable diversification of rural activities in the secondary and tertiary sectors has taken place during the last two decades, in some regions resulting in the creation of a fabric of rural industrial enterprise. In social terms, this change is reflected in the growing aspiration of rural populations to play an active role in the life of their communities. Given these economic and social trends, governments no longer regard agricultural policy as the only strategy conducive to the development of rural areas. The promotion and encouragement of local initiative and entrepreneurship are increasingly looked upon as ways of turning to advantage the natural, human and economic resources of rural areas.

Agro-food processing is not necessarily specific to rural areas, nor is it perforce the first link in their industrialisation. However, since at least at the first stage processing is an extension of agricultural production, wherever favourable market conditions and potential entrepreneurship exist processing plants can become installed and form part of the industrial fabric. In this connection, the rise of the tomato-processing industry in Portugal, has demonstrated clearly the socio-economic repercussions that result from the introduction of industry in certain rural areas.

Agro-food industrial establishments, whether or not they belong to large companies, are generally modest in scale when compared to those of other industrial sectors. This is why it is easier for them to adapt to the rural environment. In some instances, as in the case of the cheese factories in certain regions of Italy, they find their place in a traditional local culture which they help to preserve. This enables them to fit in better with the rural environment, facilitates their integration in the local economy, and enhances their prospects of survival.

The existence in rural areas or close to these areas, of either active markets for the supply of raw materials or commercial outlets for final products is indispensable to ensure the profitability of local agro-food establishments. Where processing is based on bulky or highly perishable raw materials, location in the rural area will clearly be attractive to processing firms. Where such factors are not important, entrepreneurs may still be tempted to choose a location in a rural rather than an urban area. In either case, processing establishments can generate much needed employment (both directly and indirectly) in rural areas.

Within the long-term perspective of rural development, the problem which faces public authorities is that of determining the most efficient and profitable ways to support the agro-food industries. They often find that they have to undertake industrial analyses of projects so as to establish and justify their decisions to grant aid. A frequent difficulty they meet is in seeking to promote a climate of trust between themselves and firms, and to maintain a dialogue. There are several ways to ease the situation. One is to work through semi-public bodies involving both government representatives and entrepreneurs. The Institute of Agro-Food Industry Development (Institut de Développement des Industries Agricoles et Alimentaires, IDIA) in France is one such body and its functioning represents an interesting example of the application of this method. Through such bodies, public authorities can extend financial support to potentially viable agro-industries. Industrial viability can also be promoted through the improvement of the infrastructure in the rural area.

The intervention of public authorities cannot be undertaken indiscriminately. The creation of excess capacity must be avoided. The experience of the EEC in this respect is interesting. The Commission adopted for its ten Member countries measures relating to production, processing and commercialisation of agricultural products in order to remedy structural deficiencies in underprivileged regions. The objectives of these measures are as follows:

- to encourage, through a series of aid measures, the launching of producer groups whose task is to guarantee a sufficient supply of standardized products for their clients;
- to enable firms, dealing with the processing and/or marketing of these products to modernise their operations by offering them investment subsidies.

In order to ensure that overcapacity is not created, the Commission requires Member States to draw up a regional development programme. This programme ensures that the necessary links between growers, the processing industry and market enterprises are established. The most affected sectors are milk, fruit and meat. The implementation of this programme has revealed the large investment needs of the food industry. It was recently decided that projects falling within the objectives of the Common Agricultural Policy would be given first priority and that any form of grant would be denied to intervention products or to products for which large refunds are granted. However, exceptions in favour of particularly disadvantaged areas were made. The number of programmes and projects submitted currently exceeds financing possibilities. All these incentives help those food industries, which in time, should develop autonomously without needing further investment grants, to begin their "take-off" in disadvantaged areas.

Public authorities should not be expected to shoulder the responsibility for the support of industrial structures over a long period of time. In the longer run the survival of the processing industry in rural areas can only be ensured by the existence of markets for its products, by the entrepreneurial ability of management, the productivity of the resources utilised and the flexibility and promptness of firms to adapt efficiently to changing market conditions.

E. FUTURE DIRECTIONS FOR PUBLIC POLICY TOWARDS THE FOOD INDUSTRY

General Observations

A basic issue raised during the OECD Symposium was that of the appropriate role of public authorities. In the opinion of food industry representatives, food and agricultural policies focus almost entirely on farmers and ignore the problems of the processing industries. The overall "food policy" approach, which was strongly supported by consumers, was viewed to be valid but difficult to put into practice(9). The food industry recognises its place in the agro-food chain, but stresses its links with other industries and also wishes to be considered within overall industrial policy. Governments have differing conceptions of the degree and the ways in which they should intervene in the sector. However, improving the transparency of price formation in the agro-food system, preventing the abuse of market power, protecting the consumer and creating structures for communication and, where appropriate, co-operation between all the economic agents concerned are widely recognised as appropriate government functions. With regard to state aids to the food industry, which are provided by many countries and by the EEC, these should be subject to strict economic criteria of selectivity and regarded as temporary rather than permanent measures. The principles underlying positive adjustment policies should also apply to the food industry.

Future policy directions

The agriculture and food industry sector remains heterogeneous and continues to encompass diversified sub-branches with features of their own. Two broad structures can however be identified:

a) primary processing industries having strong links with agricultural production;

b) secondary processing industries handling semi-finished products obtained from primary producers, and forming a part of the manufacturing sector rather than an extension of the agricultural sector.

Insofar as the food industry acquires more of the oligopolistic characteristics of the manufacturing sector, its relations with the agricultural sector as the

---

9. See OECD, "Food Policy", Paris 1981, and associated country reports.

supplier of raw materials will continue to change. One of the main questions in defining a framework of action for the food industry is whether it should be treated as a component of the manufacturing sector or as an extension of agriculture. There is also the question as to whether government policy towards the food industry should continue to be largely reactive i.e. designed to deal with particular problems as and when they arise, or whether a longer-term and more pro-active approach needs to be adopted.

Over recent decades the objective of policies and measures in support of the food industries has been to encourage the growth and efficiency of the sector. In the future this objective will need to be made compatible with other objectives, be they economic, social or in the general public interest, such as:

- broad economic objectives: economic growth, financial stability, improved balance of payments, full employment and job security, control of inflation;
- objectives as to the general economic performance of the food chain in particular the distribution of economic benefits among the economic actors - producers, distributors and consumers;
- social objectives such as a balanced regional policy and the development of rural regions, consumer and environmental protection, and the quality of life.

Prior and continuous appraisal of action

In view of the objectives defined above, the main question for the authorities is to determine what policy responses if any they should adopt towards the changes currently underway in the food industries. It would appear to be desirable for governments to formally evaluate the benefits and the costs associated with alternative policy responses to these changes. Some government measures may be essential, perhaps temporarily, but it would seem advisable to assess their cost. Similarly, continuous appraisal of the effectiveness of measures would ensure efficient use of public funds.

Structural adjustments

Two attitudes to structural change can be identified in OECD Member countries. One is to rely on the market mechanism and to adopt largely laissez-faire policies. Within this framework governments endeavour to limit effects detrimental to the general interest created by structural change e.g. through measures to counter over-concentration (anti-trust and anti-cartel legislation) or to encourage mergers in some sub-branches so as to achieve economies of scale and thus reduce costs. The more interventionist approach (e.g. in France) is to use a series of measures including guidance or control in the form of a medium-term development plan.

Economic forces are pushing the food industries towards concentration and product differentiation. The authorities will need to frame policies in the light of this trend. Major questions are: whether concentration or its effects should be controlled and if so how this should be achieved; what attitudes should be taken towards technological development; and the balance that should be struck between consumer protection and the freedom of the consumer.

The overall objective should be to facilitate the development of enterprises which are competitive or capable of becoming so, at the lowest possible cost to society.

The need to innovate is an increasingly essential factor in the viability of food product manufacturers, particularly since market advantages created by technology are relatively short-lived. The large firms and especially the multinationals(10) are committing substantial resources to research and development. Small and medium-size firms are making little or no effort in this area. This is one more aspect of non-price competition. The sums devoted to R & D by enterprises in the sector as a whole are modest in comparison to other branches of industry.

This situation could be improved if expanded efforts were made to co-ordinate research and development through co-operative research structures involving industry, trade associations, consumers and governments (e.g. as in the Land Grant University System of the United States or the "Collective Research Centres" in the United Kingdom). Through such a structure the results of research could be disseminated to small and medium-sized enterprises.

Policies to improve competitive conditions

In the United States and in Europe, especially in some of the EEC countries, legislation on company

---

10. Unilever employs 750 research workers, representing 25 per cent of the total number of research staff in all EEC food companies.

mergers has been enacted to curtail exploitation of market power. Government policies diverge in this field. Merger legislation in many European countries aims mainly at preventing the creation of monopolies through mergers, whereas the stricter United States legislation aims to prevent the formation of highly concentrated oligopolies. In both cases the intensity with which laws are applied depends on the views of the government of the day. Neither the United States legislation nor the more recent legislation of the EEC and certain of its member States have significantly curbed the trend towards excessive industrial concentration of the last two decades. Within the EEC, it is believed that the application of the rules of competition has helped to keep food industry structures flexible, and that the mechanism of competition is tending to operate normally within the sector. Similar rules to prevent excessive concentration exist also in other OECD countries. There is a need for further research on the application of the rules of competition in the food sector.

Other government action to encourage competition has not always met with success. The experience of the Robinson Patman Act(11) in the United States shows that to legislate on transactions may be ineffectual and even counterproductive. On the other hand, the use of published price lists may help to reduce the large price variations for identical goods, which are common in some European countries.

The evolution of government policies and the degree to which they converge or diverge internationally over the next ten years will have a considerable influence on the structure of the food industry at the national and international level.

Actions affecting producers

Agricultural producers in OECD countries have relied on their economic and political leverage to defend their position within the economic system. However, the continuing decline in their economic power which has coincided, at least in Europe, with the increasing economic power of other agents in the food chain has prompted farmers to try to rationalise and strengthen their positions vis-à-vis processors and distributors. The establishment of bargaining and processing co-operatives and other central marketing agencies (especially for

---

11. This Act included a number of provisions of which the most important was to prohibit manufacturers from charging different prices to different purchasers, except where these could be justified by differences in marketing costs.

fresh products receiving comparatively little processing), the rising number of contractual arrangements to secure outlets and reduce uncertainty, and the introduction of schemes to improve quality standards and co-ordinate supplies are examples of initiatives by producers to strengthen their power in the market.

These efforts by producers to improve the marketing of agricultural products have usually been encouraged by governments; even so, co-operative ventures have had to conform with prevailing legislation on competition. This has sometimes led to conflicts between the objectives of improving the structure of the agricultural sector and strengthening competition.

Action affecting consumers

Consumer attitudes to the scope and content of food policy and the evolution of the food chain and its components are becoming clearer and more coherent. Consumer interests extend from food quality and safety to the impact of agricultural support policies on food prices. A special problem for consumers is the trade-off between freedom of choice and protection. In this connection, the role of scientific, technical and economic consumer education is particularly important as a means of guiding decisions without resorting to controls or regulations which restrict choice, raise costs and tend to disrupt the development of new products. Another concern is educational action, increasingly called for by consumer groups.

Integrating food policy with general economic policy

During recent years the possibility of developing a coherent food policy at the national level has received considerable attention. Such a policy would encompass a wide variety of measures to ensure regular and adequate supplies and an acceptably broad range of wholesome food products, distributed by an agro-food chain in which the interests of consumers, processors and distributors as well as of farm producers were equitably balanced. In its broadest form, food policy would take account of the economic and social implications of agricultural production which were examined above in the context of rural development.

A key factor in the evolution of the food industry will be the extent to which further internationalisation is allowed to develop. The natural tendency will probably be towards greater foreign investment and international trade. However, the introduction of protectionist measures to shield national industries from competition and to encourage further domestic processing could curb this tendency. The efforts being made by certain countries to offset sluggish demand by promoting exports may also prompt protectionist reaction by other trading partners. Internationalisation and the possibilities of increased protectionism are also subjects of concern to the developing countries.

The role of governments in moderating the relationships between the various agents in the agro-food chain encompasses a number of different fields: health policy, agricultural policy, trade policy, various social and environmental objectives, competition policy, rural and regional development problems, and macro-economic considerations including inflation and unemployment. The derivation and implementation of an overall policy which ensures consistency between these disparate components may be complex. Nevertheless, it is important to be aware of the interdependences in policy in order to maintain an acceptable balance between the various interests within the food system, and at the same time maintain a dynamic relationship between this system and other sectors of the economy.

The growing international mobility of resources and food products highlights the need to strengthen the multilateral framework of these relationships. It is necessary to develop and adopt a more global approach to such problems as competition policy, standards for product quality, labelling, additives, descriptions, etc. along the lines, for example, of the Codex Alimentarius. Equally, there is a need for more refined and standardized analytical techniques with which to arrive at a better understanding of the national and international implications of the changing relationships between farmers, food processors, distributors and consumers.

In view of the growing complexity of the agro-food system, an important objective should be to achieve consistency in policy formulation at both the national and international levels. Such consistency is necessary both with respect to the regulation of the relationships between the various components of the chain and to ensure that the policies implemented for the agro-food industries are in harmony with economic and social objectives at the national and international levels.

Part II

CONSOLIDATED REPORTS PRESENTED BY THE OECD CONSULTANTS FOR THE FOUR THEMES OF THE SYMPOSIUM

DETERMINANTS OF STRUCTURAL ADJUSTMENT IN THE FOOD INDUSTRIES

by

Mr. J. M. Connor
Economic Research Service
United States Department of Agriculture

INTRODUCTION

The higher-income countries that are members of the OECD are no longer undergoing such a radical transformation that it should be termed economic development. The shares of the contributions to national income made by the major sectors of the economy (agriculture, manufacturing, etc.) change only very slowly from year to year. Mature, industrialised economies may change very little at the level of the national economy, but at the level of the sector or industry rather fundamental shifts often occur, particularly if the time frame is extended to one or more decades. This process is called "structural adjustment".

Structural adjustment is conceptually quite similar to what industrial-organisation economists term "changing market structure", albeit somewhat broader. The structure of a market is, by definition, those market-wide features that do not measureably change in the long run, particularly those elements of a market that may affect long-run economic performance. It was Bain who identified the trinity of elements currently accepted as the major elements of market structure - the number and size distribution of firms, the extent of product differentiation, and the height of barriers to entry or exit from a market (Scherer 1980). The long run was usually defined as a period extending beyond one business cycle, say, five to ten years.

Industrial organisation economics is barely four decades old as a separate field of economic science. Until recently, data availability generally constrained industrial organisation analyses to cross-sectional studies. However, in some countries data series extend back through time far enough to make feasible longitudinal studies of market structure. In the United States, for example, relatively consistent data are available on manufacturing plant numbers, plant locations, employment, and product class sales at roughly five-year intervals from 1899-1977. Sales concentration ratios are available at Census years beginning as early as 1935. Consistent data have been published annually on advertising expenditures (an important indicator of product differentiation) and industry profitability since at least 1950. While market structure data series may be more comprehensive in the United States than in most other countries, they may be a harbinger of things to come in other nations.

Not only are longitudinal studies of market structure increasingly feasible, but also they may be more relevant for public policy. Government intervention in an industry is often for the purpose of accelerating, decelerating, or freezing an observed change in industry structure. For example, a country may try to slow the declining sales of an industry that is an important source of employment. Obviously, the more that is known about the causes of structural change, the more rational a policy design can be. Moreover, if economic performance of an industry is observed to be less than the desired level, it may be easier for society to induce structural change than to attempt to control performance directly.

CAUSES OF STRUCTURAL ADJUSTMENT

Industrial organisation analyses typically assume that market forms arise from the underlying demand and supply conditions, which tend to be quite stable over time. However, changes in the basic demand or supply conditions facing a sector or industry are likely to be the main source of structural adjustment. Among several possible supply-related sources of structural adjustment, I would choose the following as particularly potent:

1. The supply of <u>labour</u>: total amounts available, skill and wage levels, regional distribution, age/sex composition and other socio-demographic features, extent of collective bargaining;

2. The supply of <u>raw materials</u>, containers, and energy: total amounts available, geographic location, weather-related or other cyclic patterns, transportation and storage facilities, degree of substitution among sources and types, methods of price discovery and risk-sharing (or risk-avoidance);

3. The supply of financial capital: rates of interest, payback periods, degree of oversight by financial institutions, reliability of bond or stock markets, ease of international transfer;

4. The attitudes, norms, and goals of management and the national business community, especially relations to government, labour organisations, the financial community, and among themselves;

5. The reservoir of technology: types of processes and capital equipment available, degree of experience with different processes, R & D capacities, economies of scale in production and physical distribution, real and pecuniary economies of multiplant (or firm) operation, elasticity of substitution among factors of production.

Equally important are changes in demand-related conditions as sources structural adjustment:

6. Nature of the product: elasticities of demand with respect to price (i.e. whether a luxury or necessity) and income (i.e. whether a normal or inferior good), cross elasticity of demand (i.e. degree of consumer substitution), ease of physical differentiation, seasonality of demand, consumer versus producer good, frequency of purchase, characteristics of households demanding (especially income, age, sex, family size, ethnic background, education), characteristics of export markets, and other taste-shaping factors;

7. Marketing methods and channels: separation of grocery store, food-service, government, and export channels, types of media advertising available, other types of advertising or sales promotion customary, extent of wholesale or storage by manufacturers, consumer relations, test-marketing systems, information on product or pricing decisions of rival sellers, and product pricing;

8. Public policies and social institutions affecting business: taxes, regional or national development programmes, enforcement of contracts, environmental regulations, safety and quality regulations, and antitrust-type constraints.

While the list above is not exhaustive, it would probably be considered moderately comprehensive by students of economic development or structural adjustment. However, I believe that to stop with the eight groups of demand-supply factors above would be a serious error given the prevailing market structures in OECD countries.

Specifically, the eight factors listed above would be adequate in a sector where perfect competition reigned and all power rested in the hands of a representative, neutral, and disinterested government. Where private interest groups exercise a degree of market power, however, additional factors may influence the rate and direction of structural change. Labour, management, buyers, or suppliers may each or all possess discretion to influence prices, quantities, or product design. In such an environment, what I will term _feedback effects_ can have substantial and predictable impacts on structural change. The consideration of feedback effects on market structure is one of the original insights of industrial organisation theory, but I believe it has been generally overlooked in previous discussions of structural adjustment.

The two main sources of feedback are from collective industry _conduct_ and market _performance_. The competitive strategies of major firms can easily alter their industry's structure, though it is not always an intended effect. Pricing strategies are one obvious mode of conduct that can affect industry structure. If, for example, a dominant firm prices so as to maximise short-run profits, this is likely to lead to an erosion of its market share through entry of new firms. However, a dominant firm may choose to maximise long-run profits with a "limit pricing" strategy that can effectively prevent market entry, particularly if other barriers are present. Predatory pricing, on the other hand, will reduce the number of firms in a market. Other forms of oligopolistic price co-ordination - cartels, overt collusion, basing-point pricing, focal-point pricing, price leadership - generally have ambiguous effects on market structure. Such pricing co-ordination is generally more important in industries with homogeneous products.

Non-price oligopolistic strategies probably have a greater influence on market-structure change than pricing behaviour. Product differentiation effects can segment markets; _ceteris paribus_, this will significantly reduce the number of firms and raise true levels of concentration. Most advertising and promotion activities involve economies of scale that can raise barriers to entry for potential competitors; moreover, the often large introductory advertising campaigns for new products could constitute a substantial absolute-capital barrier to entry. Finally, marketing a proliferation of products can so crowd a market that profitable introductions of new products becomes unlikely.

Inventive and innovative activities should also affect market structure changes. Research and development is usually carried on in a secretive manner, so discoveries of new products should destabilize co-ordinative arrangements among sellers. Similarly, the adoption of novel cost-reducing processes will introduce disparities in cost of production among sellers, make price-cutting possible by early adopters, and lead to fluctuating market shares; while the ultimate effect on concentration is ambiguous, a fluid market structure normally attracts entry. Technological change also can profoundly affect the boundaries of markets. Historically, one frequent aspect of technological change has been the development of new products that are highly substitutable in consumption or of new processes that raise the degree of substitution in production. Increases in substitutability on either side of the market imply that markets that were formerly distinct become combined; _ceteris paribus_, market concentration is lowered. It should be noted that in a tight oligopoly situation there may be strong incentives on the part of the firms benefiting from joint profit maximisation to refrain from implementing cost-reducing or substitution-increasing technologies.

Finally, the investment strategies of firms can directly restructure markets. Horizontal mergers are the outstanding example of concentrating business conduct. Even in a country with a strong antimerger policy, significant exemptions usually exist to the general ban on horizontal mergers. Conglomerates have several business strategies open to them that single-industry firms do not - cross-subsidisation of lines of business or geographic areas is one such option. Also, conglomerates, like large nations with many points of international contacts, may solidify market structures because of their reluctance to act aggressively in one line of business out of fear of retaliation in another, more vulnerable line of business. Vertical investments often have considerable impacts on pricing patterns, but the direct effects on changing market structure are difficult to trace. In industries that are highly monopolistic, firms benefiting from market power will have strong incentives to market investments that protect their monopoly positions. Such rent-seeking investment behaviour generally is aimed at raising barriers to entry. An example is investment in additional plants that results in over-capacity, but that enhances the threat-credibility of the investing firm.

Overall, I would judge that the influence on structural adjustment of performance outcomes is somewhat weaker than the influence of conduct just discussed. Allocative inefficiency might be expected to slow the growth of monopolised industries relative to more competitive ones, but among the food industries such long-run shifts are difficult to detect. Similarly, allocative inefficiency among some firms or brands in a market may cause consumer preferences to shift to products with lower prices, but product differentiation may moderate or even reverse such expected shifts. In industries producing homogeneous or producer goods, relative price enhancement probably do lead to the expected inter- and intra-industry shifts.

Technical efficiency is another element of performance, and three types may be distinguished: suboptimal capacity, excess capacity, and X-inefficiency (see Siegfried and Wheeler 1981). Research on these topics is really in its infancy, but some tentative findings are available. Studies in the United States and United Kingdom indicate that roughly one-half of industry output originates from plants smaller than minimum optimal scale (MOS), with production costs of these too-small plants being about 3 per cent to 5 per cent of higher than plants above MOS. Theory might lead one to expect suboptimal plants in more monopolised industries, and this may still be the case in smaller countries or highly differentiated industries. However, the general result from industries spread across manufacturing is that there is an inverse relationship between allocative efficiency and suboptimal capacity. The main explanation, according to Scherer, *et al.*, is that the predictability of demand in oligopolistically co-ordinated markets helps the leading firms to more rationally stage their productive investments.

The identification of truly excess capacity is a difficult task. Unused capacity at a point in time may not be excessive if input costs, input supply, or demand is cyclical, as it often is in the food industries. The consensus of studies on this topic is that *chronic* excess capacity is associated with imperfect collusion in moderately oligopolistic industries. Both highly competitive and highly monopolistic industries have a low incidence of excess capacity. No estimates of the costs of excess capacity are available.

The third type of technical inefficiency is X-inefficiency, the failure to maximise output given a bundle of inputs. The main sources of X-inefficiency appear to be lack of information on best input combinations and utility derived by workers or managers from activities other than productivity maximisation. Several United States studies support the view that lack of competition is directly related to X-inefficiency, with the cost enhancement of monopoly averaging about 10 per cent of costs

Technological progressiveness is a third element of economic performance. High rates of technological change are likely to benefit those industries at the expense of others as long-run substitution takes place, as has been seen recently in the case of high fructose corn syrup relative to cane and beet sugar. Similarly, technological progress will increase relative demand by increasing the quality or reducing the price of existing products.

While the effects on the composition of industries is quite clear, the impact on the structure of a single industry is less predictable. It is widely recognised that the discovery of commercially valuable new products or processes is largely serendipitious. As such, it benefits firms of different sizes somewhat randomly. This should in turn foster changes in ranking among firms. While concentration may remain unaffected by firm mobility, rigid patterns of firm conduct are likely to be loosened. This sanguine prediction must be tempered with the observation that highly successful small firms quite quickly become the objects of often irresistible acquisition overtures.

Technological changes are most likely to influence market structure through changes at the plant level. One of the prime characteristics of changes in production technology has been the substitution of continuous-flow-methods for batch methods. Oil refining, confectionery, some bakery products, grain products, beer, and many other foods are now made on equipment whose design is borrowed from the chemical/pharmaceutical industries. Other foods are processed using assembly line techniques first developed by the automobile industry. Thus, increasing labour productivity and capital for labour substitution is unavoidably associated with increases in economies of plant scale and in specialisation of machinery. If these rates of increase exceed the real growth of an industry, pressure builds for reductions in firm numbers and rising concentration.

STRUCTURAL ADJUSTMENT OF OECD FOOD INDUSTRIES

There are a wealth of suggestions from economic theory and empirical research on the industrial sector in general as to the sources of structural adjustment. In this section, I attempt to synthesise the findings of the national case studies presented at this symposium as well as additional studies known to the author. As a rule, the economies being referred to are all moderately to highly industrialised, i.e. with one-fifth or more of the labour force engaged in manufacturing. With a few exceptions, government ownership is nil and intervention over prices or quantities to be produced in the food industries is slight. While not my intention, my generalisations are likely to be coloured somewhat strongly by the United States case.

Importance of food manufacturing

The United States' food manufacturing industries contribute about 2.3 per cent of GDP, or about 10 per cent of total manufacturing value added (Figure 1). The ratio of value added of food manufacturing to GDP is equally low in Canada, Japan, and Italy. Among the larger OECD countries Belgium, Switzerland, and France have the highest proportion(1), over about 4.0 per cent in 1975; West Germany, Portugal, Austria, Finland, Australia, Denmark and the Netherlands were all above 3 per cent, and the rest of the countries fell in between. The relative importance of food manufacturing tends to fall as GDP increases. On the other hand, the relative position of food manufacturing in the economy appears to be unrelated to per capita product (Figure 2). This appears to contradict an international version of Engel's law, except that what is probably happening is that consumers in lower income countries use more unprocessed foods or processed foods that require more preparation in the home. However, over time nearly every country reports food manufacturing relatively declining.

Numbers of companies

Japan has the largest number of food companies, over 70,000 in 1977, including many thousands of small establishments making such traditional products as processed kelp, fish products, soy sauce, rice crackers, sake, tea, and tofu. Establishment numbers dropped by about 1.1 per cent per year during 1965-77. Except for Japan, the number of food processing firms recorded in the most recent censuses is roughly proportional to the size of the sector. The United States had about 20,000 firms, the United Kingdom about 5,300, Canada about 3,800, and West Germany 4,900. Another universal trend is a fairly rapid decline in food manufacturing firm numbers. In the United States they diminished at the average annual rate of 2.4 per cent (1947-77); in Canada by 3.5 per cent (1970-78); in West Germany by 1.7 per cent (1958-78); and in the United Kingdom by about 0.9 per cent (firms with 100 employees or more only). The number of food firms dropped markedly relative to the total number of manufacturing companies in all countries except the United Kingdom. Food firms most recently accounted for about 7 per cent of all manufacturers in the United States, 12 per cent in Japan, 11 per cent in West Germany, and 6 per cent in the United Kingdom.

---

1. Yugoslavia's ratio was reported to be 4.7 per cent. The USSR also reports a high ratio (4.3 per cent), so the figures from socialist countries may be affected by different principles of national accounting. Ireland and New Zealand report the highest ratios - over 5 per cent.

Figure 1 **RELATION OF VALUE ADDED IN FOOD MANUFACTURING TO GDP, 1975**

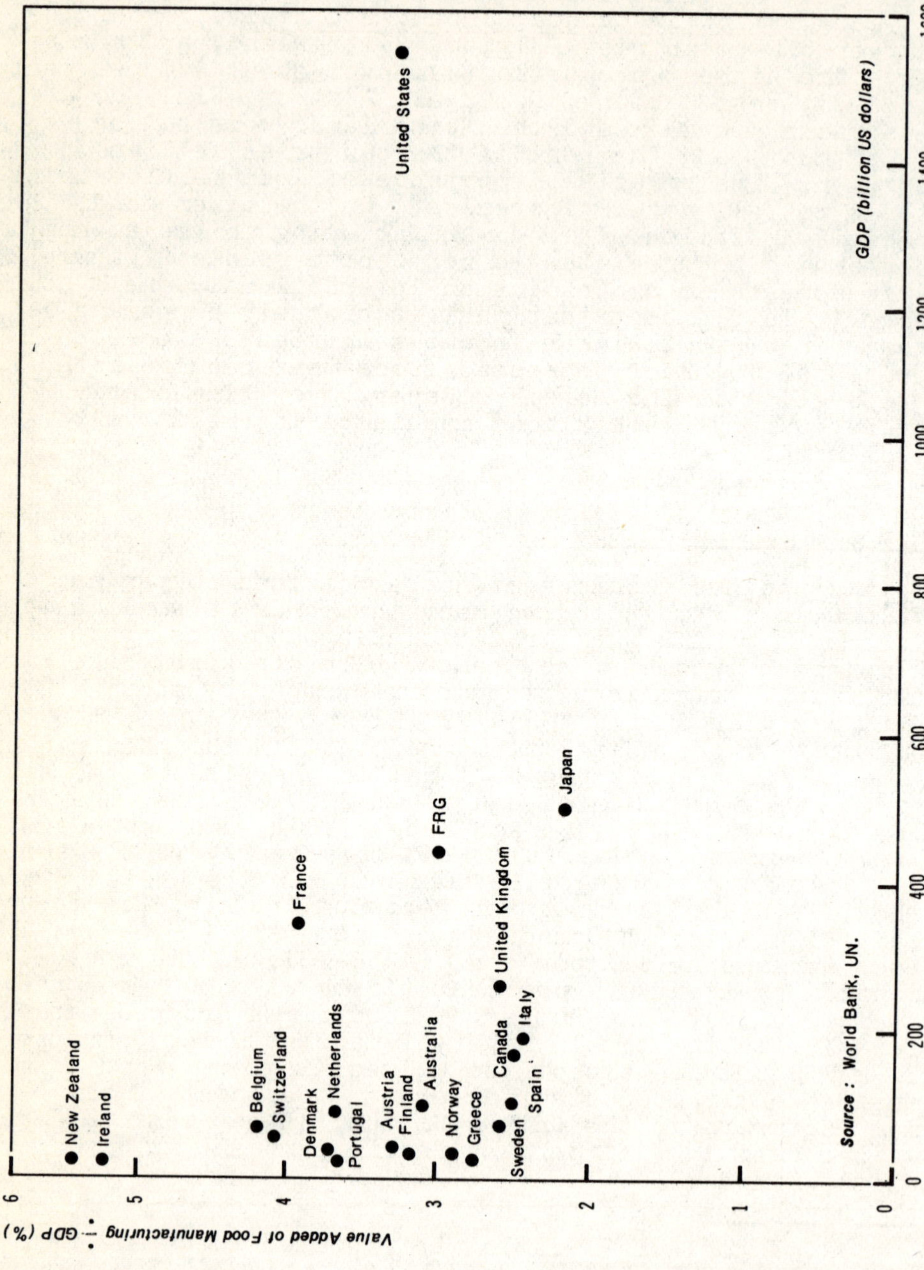

Figure 2. **RELATION OF VALUE ADDED OF FOOD MANUFACTURING TO GDP PER CAPITA, 1975**

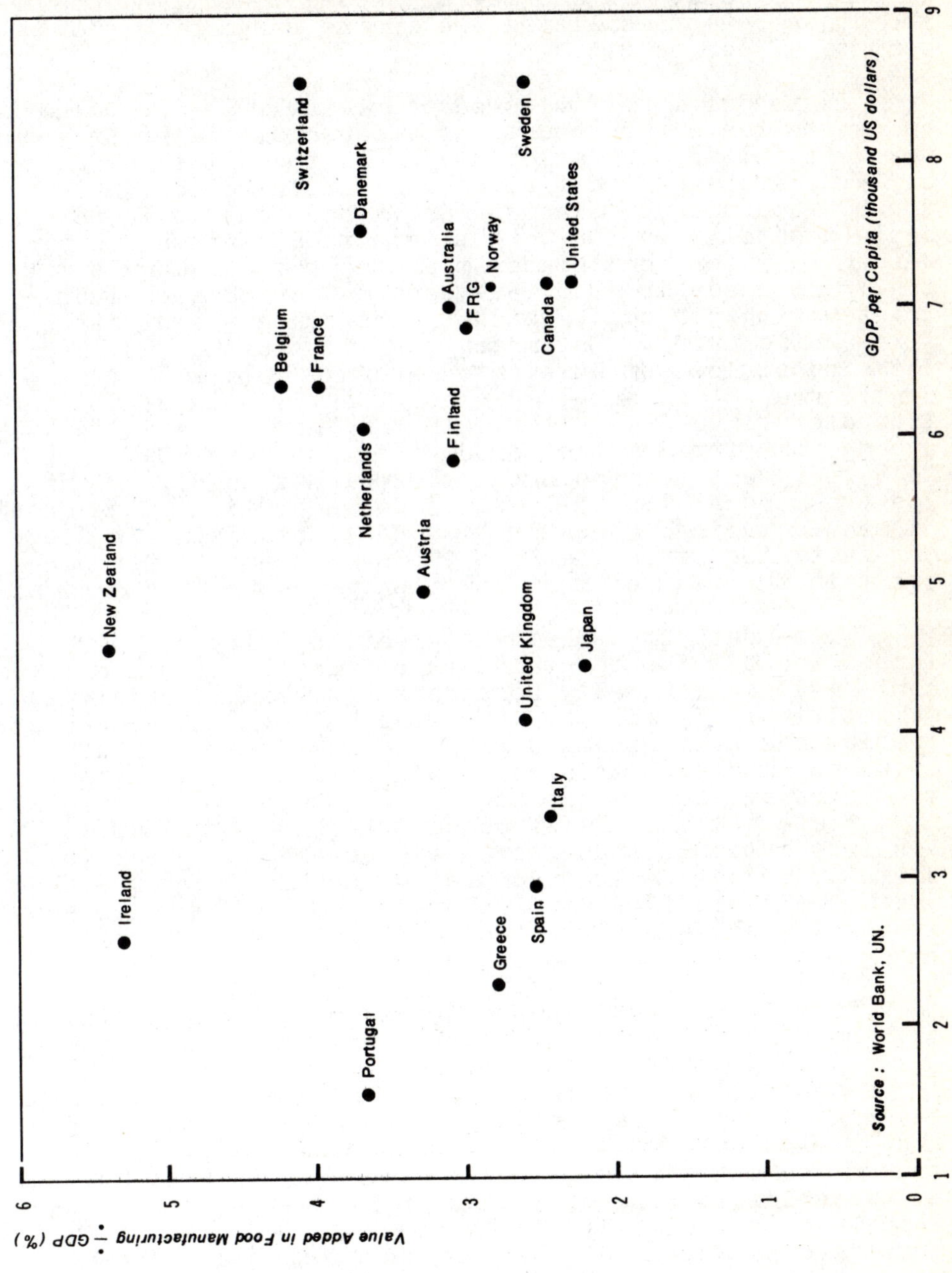

Concentration

Table 1 contains data on the position of the 100 largest industrial firms in six OECD countries. Based on sales or value added, aggregate concentration is lowest in the United States and may be second lowest in Japan; the other countries listed are in the range of 41 per cent to 47 per cent.

It is difficult to compare precisely levels of market concentration across countries because of different industry definitions and ratios used. In the United Kingdom in 1977, average five-firm concentration ratio (CR5) for 60 food product classes was 71 per cent to 74 per cent (depending on the weighting method); these averages were 6 to 9 per cent higher than the rest of manufacturing. In Canada in 1978, average CR4 for 18 food industries was 55 per cent, which by inference was higher than all manufacturing. Estimates for 11 selected West German food industries put unweighted average 1975 CR3 at 57 per cent (or a CR4 of about 62-63 per cent), with significant increases since 1960 noted. In the United States in 1977 average CR4 for 130 food product classes was 50 per cent to 54 per cent (depending on the weights used), which was about equal to the level of concentration in the rest of manufacturing; concentration has been rising in food manufacturing since the late 1950s, whereas it was constant in the rest of manufacturing.

These data show that the great majority of food industries of OECD countries exceed levels of sales concentration generally considered to lead to vigorous competition. In all the countries except Canada, concentration has been rising during the last two or three decades. The existence of local markets in food means that some of the average concentration figures quoted understate true levels of concentration. Adjustments for international trade, on the other hand, appear to slightly reduce real concentration levels from published ones. However, food manufacturing appears to be of about average or above average concentration compared to other major manufacturing groups.

Many of the same industries seem to have relatively high concentration in different countries. For example, most of the beverage industries seem universally high in concentration. Coffee, tea, chocolate drinks, instant beverage powders, soft drinks flavourings, wine, beer, and spirits have very high sales concentration ratios, though there are a few exceptions: beer in West Germany and wineries in wine-exporting or wine-importing countries. Also generally highly concentrated are highly processed packaged convenience foods, such as canned soups, infant foods, frozen dinners, breakfast cereals, biscuits, chocolate confectionery, canned milk, instant potatoes and soups, ice cream, and margarine. By contrast, industries producing less processed or commodity-type foods are more atomistic, for example, the meat, poultry, fish, fruit and vegetable canning, sugar confectionery, and grain milling (except in the Netherlands). There are a few undifferentiated foods that are relatively highly concentrated in most countries: sugar, oil processing, and wet corn milling (starch); perhaps large economies of scale are important in these cases. Finally, there are some local market food industries (bread, milk, soft drink bottling, feeds) or industries strongly affected by trade for which true sales concentration is typically unknown. In Canada, some states of the United States, and parts of Scandinavia, government restraints on the selling of alcoholic beverages reinforce higher levels of concentration.

One conclusion of the United States case study was that economies of scale or size rarely justify observed levels of concentration. Quite consistent with this view are the conclusions of the West German study, namely, that in three out of six selected food industries economies of scale require relatively high concentration (unless rapidly growing exports can moderate the trend, as seems to be the case in West Germany). Nevertheless, economies of scale in food manufacturing appear to be increasing, and in smaller national markets "natural oligopolies" may evolve. The evolution of concentration has been hastened by lenient attitudes toward mergers in some countries - the United Kingdom being one such case in point.

Production differentiation

The national case studies confirm that high advertising expenditures are found in several food industries. Some evidence links advertising to rising concentration. The correspondence in advertising intensities between the United States and Canada is remarkable and cannot be completely explained by foreign investment by United States food firms. Some foods seem eminently suitable to physical differentiation, packaging, and image advertising. In other industries the nature of the product is such that advertising plays little or no role in competition.

Branded foods are also supported by a wise array of supplementary sales promotion devices. Special discounts to retailers, sponsorship of sporting or youth groups, direct field salespersons, and coupons are among the most commonly used, but there are many others. In countries where TV advertising is restricted or unimportant, these methods are likely to be more widespread.

Food firm diversification

Based on the attention given the phenomenon, sales diversification has gone further in the United States and the United Kingdom than elsewhere. Yet there are striking differences. In the United Kingdom, alcoholic beverage companies have diversified heavily into leisure interests and hotels, while in the United States brewing companies remain singularly specialised. However, in both the United States and the United Kingdom, acquisitions are the major method by which food firms became diversified in sales; also, diversification is strongly associated with size of firm. Except for ownership of hotels and restaurant chains, the case studies do not detail any significant increases in vertical integration by food processing companies. The food service (catering) sector is growing more rapidly than sales through grocery stores, so further investments by food firms here might be expected in the future.

International trade

Trade in processed foods (excluding unprocessed agricultural commodities) is becoming more important to the OECD countries surveyed(2). Imports of manufactured foods exceed 10 per cent of domestic supply in Canada and the United Kingdom. Exports are relatively large for Canada and West Germany; in these cases proximity to large markets (the United States and EEC, respectively) has accounted for their large and growing export orientation. The United States and Canada (and probably West Germany) have a trade surplus in processed foods; Japan and the United Kingdom have severe imbalances in this trade, corresponding to their deficits in agricultural commodities. As measured by their domestic currencies, export orientation has increased substantially in West Germany and the United States and slightly in Canada.

Foreign direct investment

The case studies focused on inward foreign investment rather than outbound investment by national firms. It is clear that United States firms play a pivotal role in international investment flows. About half of the world's largest food firms are United States owned, though that proportion has declined during the last two decades as the food processing firms of Eastern Europe and Japan grew faster than United States firms. Foreign investment

2. In other countries which were not surveyed e.g. France and the Netherlands trade is also highly significant.

Table 1

AGGREGATE INDUSTRIAL CONCENTRATION OF 100 LARGEST COMPANIES IN SEVERAL NATIONS, SELECTED RECENT YEARS

Country	Years	Sectors Included	Size Measure	Concentration Level
United Kingdom	1968	Manufacturing	Value added	41%
Canada	1965	Manufacturing	Value added	44%
West Germany	1971	Manufacturing and utilities	Sales,	52%
			world sales,	47%
Japan(1)	1970	All non-financial	Assets	50%
Sweden	1963	All private manufacturing	Value added	46%
United States	1965-70	Manufacturing	Value added	33%
	1972	Manufacturing	Sales	32%
	1973	Manufacturing	Assets,	47%
			World assets(2)	44%

1. Affiliated subsidiaries are consolidated with parents.
2. Figure includes total assets of all subsidiaries and affiliated firms.

<u>Source</u>: Scherer (1980).

Table 2

FOREIGN TRADE AND INVESTMENT OF THE FOOD AND BEVERAGE MANUFACTURING INDUSTRIES, SELECTED OECD COUNTRIES, RECENT YEARS

Country and Year	International Trade				Foreign Direct Investments			
	Imports		Exports		Inward		Outward	
	Sales				Assets(1)			
United States, 1978-79	8.1	(3.7%)	9.4	(4.3%)	2.7	(5.0%)	7.3	(4.0%)
Canada, 1978	2.3	(10.4%)(2)	2.6	(11.6%)	-	(34.0%)	-	-
West Germany, 1978	-	-	8.9	(24.0%)	2.1	(15.0%)	-	-
United Kingdom, 1979	0.8	(16.0%)	0.3	(6.0%)	-	(12.0%)	-	-
France, 1979	40.0	(11.4%)	45.0	(12.8%)	-	-	-	-
Netherlands, 1978-80	-	-	21.0	(37.0%)	5.5	(11.0%)(3)	-	-
EEC (except Ireland), 1979	11.9	(5.2%)(4)	10.6	(4.6%)(4)	-	-	-	-

- = Not available.

1. Values in local currency in billions.

Percentages are the proportion of sales or assets of the whole domestic food manufacturing sector, except outward investment which is proportion of total foreign direct investment of country.

2. Per cent of domestic disappearance.
3. Based on sales.
4. Trade external to EEC only.

<u>Source</u>: OECD (1982)

in food manufacturing by all United States companies totalled \$7.3 billion in 1979, about 4 per cent of all United States foreign investment (Table 2). However, that United States investment accounts for roughly 40 per cent of the world total; United Kingdom companies account for about 30 per cent, Swiss firms another 15 per cent, and investors from about ten other industrialised countries own the remaining 15 per cent of the global stock of foreign investment in food manufacturing.

The United States is also in absolute terms the largest host country for foreign investment in the food industries, having surpassed Canada in the early 1970s. Yet in proportional terms, the United States has one of the smallest degrees of foreign investment in the food industries - about 5 per cent of sales. Foreign companies originate over 10 per cent of food manufacturing sales in West Germany and the United Kingdom; in Canada the ratio is over one-third. Another way of measuring foreign presence is the proportion of leading food firms that are foreign-owned. In 1975, among the top 200 United States food manufacturing companies, only 13 were foreign (non-United States) owned. By contrast, half of the 20 largest West German food firms were foreign-controlled, and seven of the top 30 United Kingdom food manufacturers were foreign. Thus, the United States (and very likely Japan) is relatively insulated from the impacts of foreign investment; however, this may not last long as rates of growth of foreign investment appear to be much higher than growth in domestic investment in the food industries.

One observation that appears consistent with the information at hand is that foreign investors prefer to purchase going concerns that are larger on average and that produce highly processed, packaged, branded foods that appeal to higher-income consumers. There is some foreign investment in wet corn milling, oil processing, and frozen fish, but it is rare in the meat, poultry, fluid milk, bread, sugar, and flour industries. These industry patterns of foreign investment are consistent with the view that the main advantage of multinational food companies over domestic ones is their expertise in selling techniques and the marketing of "new" brands (or variants of existing products). Firm-specific knowledge of advanced production technologies is not nearly so important in the food industries as it is in explaining foreign investment in machinery or electronics.

Profit performance

A rough generalisation is that the food manufacturing industries have long run profit rates during the 1970s that are about equal to or slightly above the rest of the manufacturing sector of their respective countries.

In the United Kingdom food industry, profits were also relatively high in the 1960s. In the United States, profitability has shown a secular rise that cannot be attributed to inflation or other macro-economic conditions. The inference is that market structure adjustments are the principal cause of rising absolute and relative profitability, in particular, the composition of food manufacturing industries has shifted toward those that have higher concentration and/or higher selling costs. The rising prices of agricultural ingredients (the major cost component of food processing) especially noticeable during 1972-74, led to only temporary reductions in food industry profits. In the United Kingdom study, the point was made that during the 1970s real prices of food inputs have fallen slightly while real prices for all inputs for the rest of manufacturing rose by 40 per cent. Among the manufacturing industries, food profits are relatively independent of energy price changes. Because the demand for food is less elastic with respect to income than many other manufactures, several studies have made the point that food industry profits are relatively resiliant to fluctuations in the business cycle.

Both the United States and Canadian studies provided data that showed that there is considerable variation in profitability among the food manufacturing industries. These variations persist for several time periods, though in Canada some industries' profits are strongly affected by export demand (e.g. fish products) or import competition (e.g. wineries). There are at least four convincing econometric studies of the United States food manufacturing industries that ascribe persistently high profit rates to high firm market shares, high industry concentration, and intense advertising. While these United States results may apply to an EEC-wide situation, the relative openness of most other OECD countries to international trade cautions against assuming that such relationships may hold for the United Kingdom, West Germany, or the Netherlands, for example. On the other hand, I would expect profit-market structure relationships like those found in the United States to persist in economies like Japan's or Australia's.

Food manufacturer' prices

A sharp distinction must be made between price analyses that are cross-sectional and those that are temporal. Cross-sectional analyses can examine variation in industry or product price-cost margins or price dispersion among brands. In this connection, two rather preliminary studies from the United States were cited. Both essentially confirm the results of previous cross-sectional studies of profit-market structure relationships. That is, differences in the degree of structural monopoly across food industries affect price-margins and brand price dispersion in much the same way as profits are affected. In Canada and the United States, evidence of price collusion or price leadership was presented. Thus, there is reason to doubt that interfirm profitability can be attributed to variation in firm efficiency. These are important findings, but they do not bear directly on the issue of structural change.

Most of the case studies presented data on general food price inflation, doubtless an important public issue in the 1970s in most countries. In both the United Kingdom and West Germany, manufacturers' current prices for foods outpaced changes in all manufacturing money prices during 1960-80, respectively; in the United Kingdom this was also true for real (inflation-ajdusted) prices as well. In the United States marketing costs have risen faster than agricultural product prices over the last two decades (the 1972-75 period an exception). However, it must be emphasized that none of these data or analyses have linked price changes to major structural shifts in the food industries. Economic theory would predict that food industries with market power would be prone to engage in "creeping inflation". Consumers react more forcefully to rapid upward price changes than to creeping prices. Ironically, it is in industries with the least discretion to absorb input price changes (e.g. meatpacking, poultry dressing, fish processing) that the most price variability occurs. In these industries current prices swing both ways, whereas in oligopolistic food industries prices are typically "sticky downward".

A potentially important issue in many OECD countries - the question of whether food manufacturers wield monopsony power over prices - was not discussed in most papers. Where government intervention exists over farm prices or supply or where farmers' co-operatives are in strong bargaining positions, food manufacturers' probably do not have much control over their input prices. Also, manufacturers of highly processed foods may purchase partly processed ingredients from other food processing companies which are fewer in number and more knowledgeable than unorganised farmers would be. In any case, relatively little research has been done on the extent of monopsony power.

Technological progress

Food manufacturers carry on very little R & D themselves, and the small amount generally involves little basic research. R & D expenditures amounted to 0.4 per cent of 1975 sales in the United States and about 0.2 per cent in the European Community. However R & D may be useful in locating or adopting new processes or equipment developed elsewhere that enhances productivity increases.

Data on labour productivity change from the United States show that some food industries have exemplary records, particularly those in which flow-type technologies or assembly-line techniques have been introduced. On average, United States food manufacturing has displayed labour productivity increases slightly above the rest of manufacturing. Perhaps more importantly, the food industries' rates of labour productivity change show no decline over the 1947-79 period. Canadian labour productivity in food manufacturing was shown to be approximately three-fourths that of United States levels. The precise causes of this disparity were not determined.

Productivity data are so difficult to compute that they are often of suspect quality(3). This is particularly so at the individual industry level. In the case of the food industries, one common structural change evidenced is a fairly pronounced substitution of capital for labour. As a result, even accurate labour productivity indexes are but partial indicators of technological progress. Just as qualitative improvement in food products likely understate productivity changes, failure to consider increases in capital or other inputs probably overstates the rate of technical progress. The United Kingdom study well illustrates this point. Over 1960-80, it was found that labour productivity in food manufacturing was about the same as all manufacturing; by contrast, multifactor (labour and capital) productivity change for food was nearly half the rate for all manufacturing.

Thus, the evidence on technological performance of the food industries is incomplete and mixed. There is little reason to believe that it is very different from other capital-intensive manufacturing industries. Indeed, the main source of technological change in food manufacturing is probably other non-food industries - chemicals, computers, industrial machinery, and precision control instruments. There is often a presumption that technological innovation will lead to ever larger economies of scale in production. However, inventions might as well lead to decreases in plant sizes; for example, new permeable membrane separation technologies

---

3. There are several reasons. Value added definitions often are too gross. Real output changes do not account for qualitative changes in products and require accurate price indexes. Input data are often better, but not all inputs are included and changes in the mix of inputs usually cannot be accounted for.

could transfer some dairy processing functions back to dairy farms. Moreover, managerial and spatial distribution diseconomies continue to be important limitations to multiplant economies of size.

CONCLUDING OBSERVATIONS

Structural adjustment is a complex, multifaceted phenomenon. The causes of long run change in the market structures of mature industries are just beginning to be studied. I have argued for the appropriateness of an analytic framework that allows for simultaneity rather than single-direction causation. That is, structural adjustment is determined both by changes in underlying demand and supply conditions (including government policy constraints) as well as feedback effects from industrial conduct and performance. Application of such a complex model to the food industries is a difficult but rewarding task.

My review of the case studies presented at this symposium prompts me to suggest a working hypothesis. The higher-income OECD countries' food industries appear to be moving toward a "structural convergence". By this I mean that the major dimensions of market structure are becoming more correlated between countries over time. The sales configurations of the food industries are the most obvious verification of this trend (especially if corrected for imports and exports). However, changes in the numbers of plants, numbers of firms, levels of concentrations, and extent of product differentiation also appear parallel in casually examining the data provided in these case studies. More precise verification should be possible in the future.

Such a structural convergence should not come as a great surprise, given our analysis of the determinants of change. First, by their silence on the topic, the case studies imply that the basic inputs of food manufacturing (labour, management, ingredients, energy, packaging, etc.) are not fixed in supply in the long run. National differences in agricultural supplies are for the most part levelled by international trade. Production technologies in food manufacturing are generally old enough to be nearly universal; new technology is spread through an imperfectly operating market for licenses, within multinational food firms, or by simple imitation. Finally, international "demonstration effects", travel, and the marketing efforts of transnational food manufacturers have caused a growing similarity of food tastes. Is there a single OECD capital city in which Chinese food, Canadian whiskey, or "American" chewing gum(4) cannot be purchased?

Structural convergence, if it is to occur, is incompatible with the widely divergent sets of public policies that different OECD countries apply to their food industries. West Germany uses direct investment subsidies to aid in the building of larger plants, while the United States approach has been to subsidise the establishment of small firms. The United States has a "tough" merger policy that allowed 15 per cent of the assets of all food firms to be acquired during 1948-68; the United Kingdom we are told has a "lenient" merger policy, yet the effect seems proportionately far milder. The United States has few controls restricting foreign investment, while Canada has recently established a screening board for foreign investments that has great discretion over individual investments. The Common Agricultural Policy of the EEC is held in one paper to have no lasting effect on market structures, while modest Canadian trade barriers and marketing boards are judged a major hindrance to good performance. Measures to improve technological performance are not discussed, though it is repeatedly mentioned as a matter of public concern.

I do not know whether harmonization of national policies affecting the food industries of the OECD countries is desirable. Perhaps the trend toward structural similarities will proceed in spite of government policies. If there were no signs that at least some food industries were evolving into oligopolies, a laissez-faire policy might be optimal. But given the evidence that some food manufacturing markets are failing, government intervention can improve economic performance and raise social welfare.

The national policies explained in the case studies appear to justify OECD concerns that there are multiple goals, some of them conflicting, being sought by numerous national agencies serving diverse interest groups. This may lead to a situation of fragmented responsibilities, stalemates between opposing forces, and festering economic problems. But it is the role of a political system to balance or arbitrage among the contending interest groups by finding acceptable trade-offs. Implicit in the social determination of trade-offs among goals are different weights or values given to each goal.

Few countries, if any, have an industrial policy specifically for the food manufacturing sector; some may consider food processing as part of a comprehensive

---

4. Really a Mexican habit learned by Americans soon after the Mexican-American War of 1845.

food policy. My own view is that the problems related to structural adjustment have a more direct connection with general industrial policies than with the upstream (agricultural) or downstream (retailing) segments of the food system. Moreover, I see few trade-offs among the simultaneous goals of unhindered international trade, monitoring and control of restrictive business practices, promotion of efficiency and progressiveness by public fundings of basic research, and temporary subsidies for viable potential competitors. From the perspective of industrial organisation economics these are complementary policies. Imports enlarge markets, thereby reducing national concentration. Exports permit all economies of scale to be achieved as well as reaping the benefits of comparative advantage. Competition reduces technical inefficiency, ensures allocative efficiency, and maximises growth through full employment of all resources. Public funding of basic research enhances dynamic efficiency, but applied industrial research is best done by the private sector because the patent system, by permitting innovators to capture rents, provides an efficient reward system. Subsidies to small businesses or infant industries can help lower barriers to entry in oligopolistic industries. These measures should lead to a well performing food manufacturing sector. Because this sector has the greatest potential for monopolisation, a highly competitive food industry will improve the chances for a smoothly functioning food system.

BIBLIOGRAPHY

Asian Productivity Organisation. *Asian Food Processing Industries*. Tokyo: Asian Productivity Organisation 1978.

Buchholz, H. E. and E. Schmidt. *The Impact of the Common Agricultural Policy on Food Processing Firms*, in OECD (1982).

Connor, John M. *Structural Adjustment of the Food Industries of the United States*, in OECD (1982).

Determinants of Structural Adjustment in the Food Industries, in OECD (1982).

Ewenczyk, B. *L'ajustement structurel des industries agricoles et alimentaires en France au cours des vingt dernières années*, in OECD (1982).

Gorecki, Paul K. *Structural Adjustment in the Canadian Food and Beverage Sector*, in OECD (1982).

Grosskopf, Werner. *Structural Adjustment in the Food Industries of the Federal Republic of Germany*, in OECD (1982).

Horst, Thomas. *At Home Abroad: A Study of the Domestic and Foreign Operations of the American Food-Processing Industry*. Cambridge, Mass.: Ballinger Publ. Co. 1974.

Klein, E. *Aspects of Food Industries in the Netherlands: Structure and Government Policy*, in OECD (1982).

Linda, Remo. Concentration and Competition in Food and Drinks Manufacturing and Distribution, in H.W. de Jong (ed.), *The Structure of European Industry*. The Hague: Martinus Nijhoff. 1981.

Organisation for Economic Co-Operation and Development (OECD). *The Adjustment of and Challenges Facing the Food Industries in the 1980s*, a symposium held in Paris, France, January 1982.

Scherer, F. M., *et al*. *The Economics of Multi-Plant Operation*. Cambridge, Mass.: Harvard University Press. 1975.

Industrial Market Structure and Economic Performance. Second Edition. Chicago: Rand McNally. 1980

Siegfried, John J. and Edwin H. Wheeler. Cost Efficiency and Monopoly Power: A Survey: *Quarterly Review of Economics and Business* 21: 25-46. 1981

United Nations, Centre on Transnational Corporations (UN-CTC). *Transnational Corporations in Food and Beverage Processing*. New York: United Nations. 1981

Watts, B. G. A. *Structural Adjustments in the United Kingdom Food Manufacturing Industry Over the Past Twenty Years*, in OECD (1982).

CHANGES IN THE RELATIONS BETWEEN FOOD PROCESSING AND AGRICULTURAL PRODUCTION, FOOD DISTRIBUTION AND CONSUMPTION

by

Mr. J. A. Burns
Department of Agricultural Economics and Management
University of Reading, United Kingdom

INTRODUCTION

While Theme I has concentrated on the structural adjustments taking place in OECD countries at the manufacturing stage of the food chain, Theme II considers the whole food sector from farmer to consumer, with particular emphasis on the relationships between food processing and other agents in the system. Sadly although the amount of research into food market structures is slowly improving in many OECD countries, with the United States providing an excellent lead in terms of information now available, the bargaining and co-ordinating activities between stages in a total production process like the food chain remains relatively under-researched and poorly understood.

There are few theories that lead to generally accepted results concerning relationships between different stages of production, but some framework of analysis can be gleaned from the work of industrial economists and from case studies. Such a framework might begin with the basic economic conditions and competitive structures at each stage, which lead on to an understanding of the relative sources of market power held by buyers or sellers along the chain. Attention may be focused on price or non-price elements, and questions raised concerning the distribution of gains (or losses) along the production chain, including the major issue of whether or not price reductions obtained at some stage (for example, retailing) are passed on to consumers. Where the system appears to perform inadequately, or involves inequitable distribution of returns, governments may intervene with the objectives of improving efficiency or altering balances of market power.

BASIC CONDITIONS AND STRUCTURE

A review of the fundamental environmental characteristics of the food sector has been made under Theme I, and many aspects are of significance for the interrelations between agents. Important among these factors is the nature of the demand for food. For OECD countries with high income levels, further economic growth rarely leads to increases in food consumption, except through income redistribution and improvements in the standards of living of the relatively poor; and food expenditure grows principally by the substitution of higher quality processed foods for unprocessed and inferior quality items, and by increased consumption of food outside the home. Although traditionally agricultural economists have viewed these tendencies as of concern for the farmers' comparative position in the economy, the impact of the sectoral decline can be noted at many stages. In order to maintain relative positions in the economy, in terms of both real income per employee and return on capital, numbers of producers decline at the farming, manufacturing and distribution stages, and capital is substituted for labour where technical or economic advantages occur. This in turn creates, particularly at the food manufacturing level, an industry with a high proportion of fixed costs and specialised inputs that need to be operated at near-capacity if average costs are to be contained.

This is not to say that the food system is devoid of growth, since there are consistent shifts in consumers' expenditure towards food with higher service components, although patterns of food expenditure by broad product category tend to stay relatively stable. One implication of both the shifts in the patterns of preferences and the competitiveness within the food system is that changes in the proportion of consumers' expenditure accruing to different stages of the food chain may alter in favour of the marketing sector beyond the farm gate.

Supply conditions, including input availability and the state of technology, demand conditions, and feedback effects from industry conduct and market performance together give rise to an industry structure in the food system. Although continually in a state of change, sometimes very rapid, at any one time this structure will be an important determinant of interrelations. While the structure of food manufacturing in OECD countries remains diverse, with every country displaying a wide range of firm sizes in most product markets, nevertheless, over the past two decades in particular, the industries have become more concentrated, smaller in numbers and larger in average size of firms, generally wider in product range and more nationally and internationally spread in their activities. Some writers have suggested that a dual classification is necessary to distinguish these agriculturally-orientated aspects of processing from the consumer-orientated production responsible for converting commodities into packaged convenience foods (Greig, 1971). The nature of the first group is to seek reliable agricultural supplies and process them into standard products at minimum costs, maximising by-product uses, and innovating to improve quality assurance and reduce the impact of supply fluctuations; while the second aims to produce identifiable packaged goods, often highly differentiated, seeking real or apparent product innovations, using advertising and promotion to distributors and consumers to maintain or develop demand. To some extent the latter category has produced new food products, like soft margarine, extruded snack foods and fabricated meats; but their key activity is to encourage consumers to substitute convenience foods for unprocessed, replacing value added in the home with value added in the factory.

Structural changes have been apparent at other stages of the food chain in OECD countries. In agriculture, however, despite improvements in average farm size, falling farm numbers and increasing co-operation, the much lower level of market concentration which typically prevails gives rise to a fundamentally weaker bargain position in relation to first stage provisions or fresh food distributors. In particular sectors the problems may be exacerbated by the nature of the farm product. "Dairy farming is dominated by a large number of small production units, and the milk in its raw form is a highly perishable product. The perishable nature of milk not only puts a limit on its transportability but also implies the need for producers to sell or process it almost immediately after production. This characteristic, combined with the relative smallness of the production units and the time lag between the decision to produce and the market availability of the product, would tend to put producers in a disadvantageous bargaining position vis-à-vis the buyers of raw milk" (OECD, 1974). Fruit and vegetables suffer similar problems of storage and perishability, cyclical overproduction and a weak farmer bargaining position.

Turning to the basic conditions and structure in the food manufacturer-distributor relationship, there has been a more dynamic process of change, and the balance of advantage has altered over time and remains different between OECD countries. In particular many studies report a marked increase in concentration at the grocery retailing and wholesaling stage. Within the food shop sector, there have been rapid reductions in the number of stores, both grocers and specialists, independents, retail co-operatives and multiple stores.

Despite their falling numbers of outlets, multiples have taken an increasing proportion of food sales, both by the rapid increase in size of their shops, and their encroachment into all specialist food areas. Changes in consumer life-styles involving less shopping trips, facilitated by car transport and home storage by refrigerator and freezer; improved food packaging and storage characteristics; the use of convenience processed foods rather than, or in addition to, fresh produce; reduced delivery of food to consumers, especially milk and bread in most OECD countries, have all contributed to this change, while the greater price competitiveness of the larger multiple stores has been an important feature, especially during periods of poor economic growth. By contrast, many retail co-operatives and independents have lost ground in both grocery and specialist areas, although the former outlet retains a prominent position in Scandinavia and to a lesser extent in the United Kingdom; and where the latter outlets have joined into voluntary chains or have location advantages, their decline has been less rapid and those stores now remaining may be stronger. On average, specialist food stores are less concentrated in few hands than is the grocery trade, with multiples controlling smaller proportions of their individual sector turnover.

In addition to these general changes, relationships also depend on the particular structural relationships that develop. For example it has been suggested that in the past, the heterogeneous structure of the United States food manufacturing and retailing industry has led to large firms at one stage dealing with small firms at the other. Harmon suggests that developments are in train that may lead to the emergence of bilateral oligopoly relationships more typical of some other OECD countries, such as the United Kingdom and Denmark.

OTHER DETERMINANTS OF BARGAINING POWER

While structural factors will be significant in the food chain relationships, other influences, in some cases arising out of market structure and basic conditions, may play important roles. The United States case study stresses the relative significance of supplier (or buyer) to buyer (or supplier) in the manufacturing-distributing part of the food chain, although similar considerations arise between farmers and agricultural processors, as we have seen in the case of milk and horticultural products mentioned above.

At the food retailer-manufacturer stage, many studies indicate that calculation of market shares for firms in the sector fails to provide a complete picture. Retailers in particular have flexibility, both in the use of their capital for different products, and in the sources of supply they choose, while for the specialist manufacturer, the loss of a major retail chain might well reduce capacity working levels significantly. Producers may attempt to counteract this situation by reaching consumers directly, and their policies of product differentiation and advertising are designed to create consumer dissatisfaction with retailers that fail to stock the manufacturers' brands. A further possibility occurs with the diversified firm, which is able to cross-subsidise products facing severe competition or market decline at any one time. Such a policy is unlikely to be pursued indefinitely, but may contribute to the demise of smaller or weaker competitors, and certainly gives rise to poor market transparency. On the other hand, retailers have been able to counter customer loyalty for manufacturers brands by establishing their "own brands" (or private labels), where the focus of market initiative is moved downstream. Both United Kingdom and United States studies indicate a further range of measures that retailers may take that are liable to influence sales of particular items, including promotion activities, display and positioning of items in store.

A somewhat extreme measure that may be undertaken with a view to altering the bargaining relationships is full vertical integration by one firm into other stages in the chain. While there is evidence in both the United States and United Kingdom of some vertical integration activities, it is not clear whether this potential weapon has been used effectively to bargain with buyers or suppliers. However, it may be that the integrated firm gains a better understanding of other stage production circumstances, and can secure better terms with outsiders.

PRICE AND NON-PRICE COMPETITION

It is clear from the case studies, that price terms between agents in one chain merit special distinction from non-price features. In part this reflects the concerns of economists that competition focuses on pricing, and consumers clearly gain from lower prices, while non-price elements of product differentiation, advertising, services, location of outlets and so on, are aspects of inter-firm rivalry, and consumers' benefits are less easily identified or quantified.

In the relationships between farmers and processors, the pricing arrangements are influenced in many countries by policy measures undertaken to support agricultural sector incomes, and a major problem is that of market transparency: the degree to which it is apparent that consumer prices are influenced by farm price support. A second issue of price discovery arises as a consequence of the growing direct relations between farmers and processors, since remaining free markets may become smaller and less efficient indicators of equilibrium prices. Downstream, the major features highlighted in the manufacturer-distributor terms are price discrimination, whereby large retailers are able to obtain discounts from suppliers; and price variability, most noticeably manifested at the retail store. It is clear that many instances of price discrimination rely on the bargaining strength of retailers rather than reflecting true cost differences, although in the United States the latter justification is legal, while most others are not.

Non-price aspects of the relationship between manufacturers and farmers often relate to the securing of appropriate quality, quantity and timing of inputs into the processing business. While prices may successfully fulfil an information transmission role in terms of volume and quality, detailed arrangements may require contracted agreements, which may also serve to reduce market risks. Direct links have also become important in manufacturer-retailer relationships, due to changes in structure, technology of distribution, stock control and handling. Again non-price elements cover areas of product specification and development, advertising and promotion, and a broad range of business services.

MARKETING CHANNELS FOR AGRICULTURE

In order to discuss the relationships between agents at this stage in the food system, it is initially convenient to classify the routes of sale of agricultural produce in the following four main ways:

a) to commodity food processors - whose objectives are to secure a consistent supply of reliable quality inputs at minimum costs;
b) to retailers directly - especially possible where "short chain" produce such as fruit, vegetables and carcase meat are involved, and retailers' objectives are similar to (a);
c) to co-operatives or marketing boards - whose objectives are to improve the farmers' return by market segmentation, supply and grading control, bargaining power, promotion, *et al.*; and

d) to wholesale markets - where produce of varying quality may be disposed of, at a price, and merchants or agents carry out functions of grading, standardizing and disposal for end-use.

OECD countries appear to be relying increasingly on routes (a) to (c); with (d), the traditional outlet, taking a smaller proportion of the total. It is apparent that, with the scale of operation of many of the processors and retailers, their needs are best served by links with specialised farmers or farm co-operatives and groups, as important issues of variety, quality, timing of harvest and delivery, amongst others, can be resolved in contract or full integration. By contrast the uncertainty of the open market appears to provide a poor alternative, except for opportunist buying.

Encouragements to these direct links have come, for example, from technical developments in transport and the physical distribution from farmer to user. In addition, general developments in communication, improvements in vehicle design, containerisation and specialised construction, especially with regard to temperature control, have facilitated larger-scale processing, using farm products from wider areas. Agricultural sector changes that have aided transport include, in general, the increasing size of farms, and in particular, bulk storage of milk and cereals on-farm; as well as mechanisation of harvesting, drying and grading, and control of production. Transport technology has enabled the shift of some production facilities, especially meat slaughtering, closer to the agricultural producers, with the subsequent movement of primal and retail cuts to outlets.

AGRICULTURE AND FOOD MANUFACTURING RELATIONSHIPS

We have seen that two important aspects of the relationships between these two parts of the food chain operate against the farmer's position: the atomistic structure of farming vis-à-vis processors and distributors, and the dependence of producers of perishable products with long production lags on rapid disposal of their output. Government intervention has in many cases been used to improve the farmer's position, but also many farmers, despite their tenacity for independence, have sought solace in marketing co-operatives or statutory boards. However, these institutions do not provide all solutions. Some writers suggest, for example, that the traditional organisation of co-operatives results in limitations in economic strength that lead to disadvantages in the market place, unless treated favourably by policy-makers (Allen, 1974).

There are potential conflicts between managers, who see their job as maximising the performance of the co-operative, and farmers who see it as specifically serving the agricultural producer's objectives, in terms of, *inter alia*, prices and willingness to accept produce. Hence price fixing, for example, has to balance giving a favourable return to the farmer, and yielding sufficient surplus to the co-operative for capital investment, innovation and salaries for effective management. There are also problems of exclusiveness, both of farmers using the co-operative consistently, rather than reverting to other outlets for short term gains; and of co-operatives trading in products that compete with those of its farming members, for example, dairy co-operatives responding to consumer trends by handling margarine and non-dairy creamers (OECD, 1974). Where farm technology, input and output processing and marketing developments imply larger organisational units, the local co-operative has come under strain or needed to adapt in such a way that the individual farmer's voice is less well heard. Particularly when both farmers and non-farmers are involved, as, for example, in the Danish fertilizer industry co-operatives or through the French SICA organisations, the style of co-operation is rather different from the traditional.

Contractual agreements between farmers and manufacturers or retailers are often an alternative to co-operatives (or market boards) and may be preferred in countries like the United Kingdom or the United States where the farm structure is stronger in general. Particularly when considerable management and technical skill is required (for example in growing high quality seed) the good farmer may feel more in control of his own organisation and more capable of meeting exacting standards than the co-operative. In other circumstances co-operative grading and standardization schemes may be appropriate to meet contract terms.

In general contracts may be limited to "marketing arrangements" covering issues such as price, quantity, quality, timing of sale or delivery methods, be of a limited "joint venture" or "market linked" type, or provide for full "transferred management", where almost all production as well as marketing decisions are laid down in the contractual agreement (Barker, 1972). From the view of the processor or retailer such arrangements go far in assuring the flow of appropriate agricultural inputs, and in addition the system may assist in the transfer of information from consumer to farm level, for example in fruit and vegetable, or deadweight pig and cattle contracts. On the other hand it is not difficult to see the farmer's reluctance to limit decision-making on-farm, or restrict marketing options, especially when market alternatives provide comparable or occasionally better returns (Barker, 1981). Nor is the farmer's security completely assured, as it is not unknown for processors to turn to the freemarket when prices are low, finding some escape route from the contractual obligation, through, for example, quality stipulations. Competition amongst buyers for contracting farmers' products appears to remove the worst problems, but with declining numbers of processors and increased concentration, this condition is not always fulfilled. Joint venture contracts, where risks are shared between grower and processor, are a useful alternative, if satisfactory cost arrangements and mutual trust can be established. This sometimes requires the setting up of a jointly owned subsidiary to buy the farmer's output and market it to the user or retailer (Malcolm, 1981).

It may be that co-operative organisations, or government sponsored marketing bodies, have a significant role in helping establish model contracts, or contract clauses, with mutually agreed grading and quality standards for use in arrangements between farmers and manufacturers or retailers, with an improvement of security on both sides. Where government or international agricultural policies provide for market intervention, it would seem appropriate that similar grading schemes be devised, fitting the circumstances of producers and users in individual countries where necessary.

Little has been said in this section about vertical integration upstream by manufacturers into farming. This is largely because, apart from the poultry and egg markets, there seems little evidence of extensive use of this practice in OECD countries. The United States appears to have most, but even there commentators have suggested that the capital requirements and low rates of return in agriculture make investment in farming a poor alternative to contracting for manufacturers (OECD, 1979).

With contracting, forward integration by co-operatives, or the comparatively rare examples of backward integration by manufacturers into farming, a further problem may arise if a significant proportion of high quality produce is diverted from the free market, which may in extreme cases become both residual and unrepresentative, and subject to price instability around a low average.

The processes of price formation between stages may be undertaken by various means including free markets, direct negotiations, group negotiations on the basis of estimates of supply and demand, through formulae or by fixing input purchasing and output selling prices (de Vlieger). Market structure will play a part in determining which method is employed, although objectives, such as an equitable distribution of returns (in relation to costs), might influence the adoption of more formal methods such as the use of formula prices.

In all comments about the position of agriculture in the food chain, it is hard to remove the impact of government intervention, which plays a greater or lesser role in all OECD countries. Since governments support agricultural incomes by subsidies, influence supply to the market through boards or marketing orders, set minimum prices or price guarantees by support buying, deficiency payments or export restitutions, encourage co-operatives through agreeable arrangements for finance; the political power of the farming community leads to market power via government action. Objectives such as securing minimum, or improved, incomes in the agricultural sector, slowing the decline in numbers in farming, or encouraging rural development, are often approached indirectly through market forces; and in particular support of farm prices robs the market of the free working of its principal communicator, and consumers of the welfare gains that lower prices bring.

FOOD DISTRIBUTORS

It is arguable that of all changes in the food chain over recent years, the increase in market power by the major food distributors has been the most dramatic and effective. In Europe, the major grocery retail chains have so expanded in terms of their absolute size, proportion of total food sales, size of shop, reputation with consumers, and hence importance to all producers, that few manufacturers are in a relatively advantageous bargaining position. This is not just a matter of size, and market share, significant though these are. In the United Kingdom, at least, an important additional factor is that of the slow growth, or in some product markets decline, in consumer demand. This, coupled with the substitution of capital for labour in the food manufacturing industry, has led to excess capacity and hence fierce competition for retail orders, along with a willingness to produce distributors' own-brands or brand-free "generic" products.

A major consequence of the growing scale of multiple operations and their widening product scope has been the development of direct links between manufacturers, or farmers' organisations, and retailers' own central warehousing systems. Grocery wholesalers still deliver to independent stores, especially when part of the wholesaler sponsored voluntary chain, and to the catering trade, which is increasing in importance in many countries; but a greater proportion of the wholesaler's business is now through the cash and carry method. This latter has advantages of lowering transport and associated labour costs, and reducing credit difficulties. As in retailing, the grocery wholesalers have expanded into traditional specialist areas, especially frozen foods, fresh meat and fruits and vegetables.

Large retailers, especially grocery based stores, enjoy many economies of scale, including storage and stock control, transport and distribution, display, advertising and quality control, although the principal advantage is probably in their buying power and importance to the manufacturer as an outlet. While in the United States and the United Kingdom, the central buying offices of the retailing companies house the major market force, in France the commercial groupings or _supercentrales d'achat_ appear to be the focus of "real strength" (OECD, 1979). The advantageous results for the multiple retailers seem to be in two main areas:

i) prices and other terms of supply obtained on manufacturers' national brands;
ii) distributors' own brands or generic goods supplied at competitive prices by the manufacturer, possibly the national brand leader, but medium-sized firms able to meet the retailers' requirements are significant in some sectors.

The price formation process for manufacturers' established brands displays significant differences between the United States and Europe, primarily because of the legal requirements in the former country. In particular, the Robinson-Patman Act forbids price discrimination by manufacturers unless price differences are explained by cost differences with respect to buyers, or in some exceptional circumstances. List prices published by manufacturers indicate wholesale prices for their goods, with discounts related to quantity of purchase, and all purchasers deal on the same terms. In Europe, while such lists exist, they often include other features such as discounts for services, sales promotion and methods of payment in manufacturer's general conditions. In addition retailers may negotiate special terms involving rebates related to size of sales and business co-operation (Yon, 1982). Hence retailers may well pay widely different net prices for the same manufacturer's product, and in Europe this is indicated by the significant variations in retail prices shown in competing outlets.

There does not appear to be complete unanimity amongst case study authors as to the problems raised by this discrimination, although all appear to agree that legislation along the United States pattern would not be suitable to Europe. While the French contribution condemns the unspecified rebates as leading to poorer price transparency and hidden barriers to entry of new competition, the approach of the United Kingdom study is more tolerant, suggesting that retailer power to obtain unjustifiably favourable terms is more limited. Although individual producer firms may suffer in the short run, it is contended that the system as a whole is unlikely to suffer serious problems of pricing below-cost in the long run. It is also stressed that consumers decide the future structure of retailing in so far as they react to price differences that emerge between alternative outlets.

Hence manufacturers have retained relatively strong market positions in the United States, and have continued to encourage customer loyalty by non-price activities such as advertising and branding. However the growing area of distributors' own-brands and generic brand-free products has taken place where the Robinson-Patman Act is largely ineffective, as differences in specifications make products, and their prices, difficult to compare. The own-label and generic products are important too in Europe, and here, unlike in the United States, major producers tend to involve both manufacturers'- and retailers'-brand items. By refusing to produce these items for the major retailers, or wholesalers, the opportunity to use idle capacity may be lost, and rivals (large or medium-sized) may take up the option instead. Since the product becomes the distributor's brand, it matters little who supplies it, as long as specifications are met. On the other hand, this product will likely attract sales from the producer's nationally advertised brand.

With retailers' own-brands, it is clear that the balance of market power and initiative has moved downstream from manufacturer to distributor. Consumers accept the main retailers' brands in terms of quality, and new products are created for retailers as well as existing manufacturers' items approximately copied. In the United States, distributors' price information on own-brand foods is superior to producers', and retails are able to alter prices in order to adjust inventory levels in accordance with stock policy. The impact of such adjustments will be felt mainly by processors, and, in the case of items with substantial agricultural raw material components, farmers (Harman, 1982).

Vertical integration occurs both ways between manufacturers and distributors. Arguably retailers have taken over food manufacturing companies to obtain oligopoly profits, but a more important aspect has been to reduce dependence on large processors, and thus to continue the swing in balance of market power towards retailers (OECD, 1979). There is evidence of such integration in the United States, France and Denmark, and in the latter two countries, and the United Kingdom, the retail co-operatives have been most active in upstream full vertical integration. However, despite somewhat inadequate documentation, evidence suggests that manufacturer-retailer contractual arrangements have become more significant than full integration, especially in the United States (Greig, 1978).

The United Kingdom on the other hand displays a greater tendency to downstream integration by manufacturers into distribution. This is most noticeable in specialist areas, for example, meat slaughterers-butchers, and millers-plant bakers-bakery outlets, rather than in grocery trades. A major exception is Associated British Foods-Fine Fare, while other integrations appear more akin to diversification. Indeed, Unilever, the leading food firm, sold its major United Kingdom retail interests in the early 1970s, and minor ones in the late 1970s, claiming that their forward integration caused difficulties in its relationships with other retailers. Except for specialist trades and some individual firm cases, it is suspected that manufacturer downstream integration has made comparatively little impact on the power of leading food retailers in the United Kingdom.

A more limited degree of vertical integration is implied by the direct manufacturer-retailer linkage, but which may have important implications for competition, especially when the wholesale distribution function is processor owned. The example of frozen food distribution in the United Kingdom is illustrative here (MMC, 1976). In order to establish a cold chain to retailers, the major processors concerned invested in cold stores, refrigerated trucks and retail freezer cabinets. Since smaller manufacturers were unable to match the capital outlay, it was not until the growth of specialist frozen food wholesalers, and retail supermarkets and freezer centres using their own facilities, that they were able to compete effectively with the large frozen food manufacturers.

It would be wrong to imply that the small grocery or specialist retailer is necessarily finished, or will play no important role in the future pattern of shopping, rather that the position may be more complementary than truly competitive. Those stores in voluntary groups can obtain buying strength, distributors' own brands, advice on management and finance, promotion and display design; and where they enjoy locational advantages near urban or rural residential areas and provide extra services such as longer opening hours, they are an attractive alternative, especially for consumers without cars, deep freezers or the desire to shop infrequently. Specialist stores, particularly of high quality, also are likely to remain significant, although the larger stores tend to incorporate their kind within the grouping framework. These smaller outlets will continue to provide an opportunity for specialist and limited scale manufacturers to reach consumers with their established or new products. This may be increasingly the case as multiples monitor their product sales more closely through the use of article numbering and scanning, and slow-moving items are identified and excluded.

CONSUMERS

The basic characteristics of the consumers' situation on average in OECD countries is well-known, and broad introductory remarks would seem sufficient. Generally consumers have enough to eat, and income does not appear to be an effective constraint, at least on average calorie consumption. It does not seem clear what effects, if any, will arise should current macro-economic difficulties of recession and unemployment continue. Regional, climatic, and traditional variations exist, but there are converging trends in the balance of animal and vegetable source food as shown in country consumption averages (OECD, 1981). The substitution of sugar and alcohol derived carbohydrates for staple cereal sources continues, although sugar is consumed increasingly as a component of manufactured foods and drinks.

Since basic nutritional requirements are met, the utility of food is more derived from its other attributes, including: convenience, quality, variety, novelty, and health related characteristics. Hence we see in OECD countries increasing proportions of convenience foods, saving labour and leisure time in the home; more meals expenditure on food consumed outside the home; improved quality of processed foods especially in their closeness to fresh alternatives; greater variety of foods arising from the communication of regional and international tastes, and yet simultaneously closer uniformity amongst nationally produced brands, advertised and sold ubiquitously; continual introduction of new products, often related to developments in consumer durables - freezers, food mixers and processors, microwave ovens; and almost paradoxically, a greater concern with health characteristics of foods - nutritional qualities, diet related diseases, freedom from additives, or traces of herbicides and pesticides used in farming, and the related but wider issue of safety in foodstuffs.

Considering first the choice of products available to consumers, we have a number of conceptual difficulties of what constitutes a separate or new product, or what a marginal variation, brand or package change, or "product space filler" (Connor, 1981). If, as some authors claim, food firms are more concerned with marketing innovation than with production technique improvements, one might ask if the new product provides additional qualities or services demanded by consumers, or is merely aimed to create stronger product proliferation barriers to entry for potential new competitors. In the latter case, a greater competitive or product improvement may be deterred by a lesser. However, while it is easy to criticise firms for excessive new product introduction, it is difficult for producers to correctly anticipate which new products consumers actually want. There remain delicate assessment problems, since product proliferation normally will provide consumers with foods that more closely match their specific requirements, but fewer products at cheaper prices may have given higher welfare gains (Connor, 1981; Scherer, 1979).

In some respects, however, there may be opposite kinds of forces at work, since it is not just a question of what products are made by firms, since consumers buy from the choices that retailers offer for sale. With the better monitoring of sales, more or less successful products will be noted earlier, and particularly at times of slow economic growth, large retailers may limit their alternatives to one or two leading national brands, plus their own, or generic, brand. With the major multiples taking a greater proportion of food sales, this may result in some products achieving excessively long life-cycles, supported by promotion expenditure and their established places on the retailer's shelf, consumers finding a limited choice available, and new product producers unable to find outlets.

Price competition is justly praised for improving consumer welfare, but it should be recalled that food retailers normally reduce prices only on a limited range of products, seeking those that will attract customers into the shop, and hoping they will then also buy the more profitable lines. Excess capacity and retail economies of scale have increased the fierceness of price competition, and consumers appear to have greater awareness of price differences, due, perhaps, to inflation, activities of consumers' associations and investigative journalism, but a great deal of the cost of competitive price reductions is born by the manufacturers in the form of discounts demanded by retailers. This form of price discrimination and competition may well be in the short run interests of consumers, and probably the long run for the majority, but it is possible that the resultant reductions in the numbers of small food outlets may not be satisfactory to some sections of the community, for example, the old and relatively less well-off living in rural areas.

A further aspect of price to interests of consumers relates to various aspects of information. Venables(1) claims that greater transparency in price formation, leading to, for example, identification of the impact of agricultural policy measures on retail prices, or of processing and marketing costs, would improve policy-making and competition. In addition more information on local food prices would stimulate customer awareness of differences, and possibly promote greater uniformity. However this may also hasten the demise of the smaller food shop.

The increased concentration of retail buying power in the hands of new multiple stores could lead to a lessening of price competition and eventually consumers may have fewer alternative outlets from which to choose. Prevention of further merger activity beyond an agreed level of concentration might reduce the probability of this outcome, but there is the inevitable issue of what is the critical concentration level, and also the fact that many of the strongest food chains have grown internally rather than by external acquisition.

Turning to the distribution linkages, many commentators consider that the direct farmer or manufacturer-retailer chain has lowered costs, and that some inefficient wholesalers and wholesale markets have been removed or made more competitive. Particularly in the fresh food trades where grading and consumer identifiable standards have been difficult to establish, the multiple chains, in operating their links with producers, have interpreted consumer requirements, as they seem them, in very precise specifications to farmers and growers. This consumer-orientation engendered in producers is likely to prove beneficial, although there may be short run difficulties in meeting requirements and in disposal of unwanted products or by-products.

Finally, in this section, consumer interest in food quality and its health implications needs to be mentioned, although it is a complex issue, and a combination of information and misunderstanding. Basic matters, such as the immediate safety of foods, are largely beyond dispute, but exactly what evidence is necessary to inspire government limitations on or warnings about, foods with possible long term deleterious effects is hard to define precisely. Certainly consumers should be kept informed as to the most balanced overall view, and specific problems relating to particular foods. Consumers should be able to avoid any substances they do not wish to eat, and the display of information on additives and ingredients on food packages, in a simple, understandable form, would be a useful step in this

1. See Part III.

direction. Whether or not it is necessary to employ the procedure of "positive tests" of proved harmless products (Venables, 1982) is another matter, although it might well be argued that the more effective enforcement of existing regulations would be advantageous.

ROLE OF THE GOVERNMENT

At various points in the discussion so far, the involvement, and concern of, governments with agriculture and food sector activities has been noted. A wide range of policies has been mentioned, and should be thought of together as it is increasingly realised that an overall approach to food is relevant to policy-making. In particular, the impact of policies directed at one stage in the food chain on activities carried on in another should be considered, as part of the progress towards more integrated policy-making. Traditionally, although governments have been aware of the vertical linkages in the sector, the objectives of the most politically powerful pressure groups were often fulfilled in preference to those less well organised or obviously at risk. While some export orientated countries tended to provide limited support, for many OECD members, especially in Europe, agricultural communities appear to have gained most, especially when the total numbers, and proportion of population employed in agriculture were high, and the farm vote considered significant for political success.

Many agricultural support programmes aim to raise farm incomes through increasing prices. Given some response that increases supplies, the agricultural sector may become more self sufficient, and processors alter relations with existing importers, or enlarge export activities. At the other end of the food chain, these policies have obvious implications for consumer welfare, especially the low income groups, for whom food is a larger proportion of total consumers' expenditure than average, and for trading relations as cheaper imports are taxed, but they also tend to create a more or less rigid system of policitally-influenced price relatives. While this may slow the progress of economic change in the farm sector, it encourages the development of alternatives not included in the price support schemes. In turn these new raw materials or products may be taxed, banned or otherwise discriminated against, in order to maintain the status quo.

Additionally, the nature of the support scheme will affect the downstream activities. For example, if surplus output has to be stored, it may need to be converted into non-perishable forms or frozen: and hence the schemes effectively support not only farmers but pass the excess capacity of the agricultural sector on to first stage processors, (Buchholz and Schmidt, 1982). Further effects arise as supplies of intervention products are made available to manufacturers, caterers, or certain restricted consumer groups; or sold on international markets.

While price support measures are criticised, it is not necessarily in either the manufacturers' or consumers' interests to see farm prices depressed to uneconomically viable levels. Despite the pressure that competing retailers exert on prices, it is strongly arguable that consistent, good quality supply is more important than transitory price cuts. For firms using price supported inputs, compensation in the form of subsidies to ensure sales to take place at world market prices may not always work perfectly, and will necessarily involve administrative complications and costs. Moreover, in general, greater "consistency and continuity" has been urged for agricultural policy, so as to reduce uncertainties and encourage more entrepreneurship amongst those persons whose activities are closely linked to farm products.

At the farm level, governments have made attempts to promote improved marketing by the encouragement of co-operatives and agencies for the central marketing of fresh or comparatively less processed products, by structural reforms, and by improving farming infrastructure. Attempts to establish uniform grading and quality standards have not always been entirely successful, and some have argued that regulations may have restricted consumer choice (Venables, 1982). Similarly food law harmonization programmes and measures to eliminate non-tariff barriers have often encountered impediments themselves to progress. Governments may find such objectivity laudable in theory, but difficult in practice when conflicting with the interests of national pressure groups or vested interests.

A second major area of government policy concerns competition and restrictive practices, and here difficulties arise with the theoretical basis and practical implementation of legislation. Industrial economics does not supply simple guidelines as to the most desirable industrial structures or competitive activities, and although certain practices are generally deplored, in the main imprecise phrases such as "effective competition", "abuse of power" and "public interest" are employed, and case law is necessary to establish sharper definitions of what is acceptable and what is not. Moreover, economies and non-economics continue to evolve, and problems of short term versus long term interest arise, with the difficult matter of predicting competitive situations and activities into the future.

The stance of competitive policy is usually *prima facie* against concentration, but on the other hand governments have recognised, either directly or indirectly the inefficiency of fragmentation and small-scale operation in many areas. In an attempt to create a more rational use of resources - land, capital, expertise and skilled labour, they may encourage increased sizes of farms; and the creation of co-operatives, and development of commercially based marketing organisations, with the possibilities of downstream processing, storing, grading, standardization and quality control, the better use of information and negotiation of contractual arrangements. In the extreme case of marketing boards with monopoly supply, a clear conflict with competition objectives is possible, and appropriate "checks and balances" incorporated into the legislation of the boards.

It may be that the focus of policy on the food chain is especially relevant to this aspect of competition policy and rationalisation of small scale production. Many of the most difficult problems occur when imbalances of bargaining power along the chain exist; and a policy that seeks to prevent exploitation by the strong and improve the market position of the weak by encouraging reorganisation and development would be of general benefit. Of course, the practical difficulties of such a policy are not to be underestimated.

One such area in which policy measures have been attempted is price-discrimination regulations in the United States. It is clear that implementation of the Robinson-Patman Act has been troublesome and costly, and economists are divided as to the effective outcome of the pricing regulations it involves. While no European country has yet introduced similar measures, sufficient concern over manufacturer-retailer relationships in the food trades has been expressed that some suggestions have been proposed as to codes of practice or publication of price lists. The major concerns cover further concentration at the retail level, including the elimination of many small stores, and the consequent reduction in consumer choice of outlet. A related issue is of price differences for comparable products sold in the same areas. While manufacturers' price lists may help to promote consistency, greater information to consumers might induce a similar result.

In the area of macro-economic policy, conflicts may occur with, for example, inflation control and food price objectives and support to the food sector. There may be unwillingness to raise farm incomes through price support and attempts to control prices and margins at retail levels. Here the necessity of not underminding investment in the sector from low profitability is relevant, although the impact of margin controls in particular is likely to be more or less influenced by the state of competition in the retail sector. Again, dangers of rigidity in prices arise.

Unemployment considerations are, of course, basic to the support of the agricultural sector, but are also relevant to the use of competition policy, or rather, its non-use. Where dangers of severe local unemployment arise through the possible closure of large-scale food production, governments may encourage or allow mergers or restrictions on competition, to seek a slower run-down of capacity. Such difficulties may arise, for example, by objectives of increased self-sufficiency and support to home farmers making import based industries uncompetitive.

Finally, consumers' interest in the food chain comes in two main fields: competition and prices; and consumer protection and safety. With the former, the question of choice is most significant, since when they are limited in availability of products or retail outlets, consumers' interests are most likely to suffer. Choices too are best made on an informed basis, and this implies both consumer education and understandable information made available at time of purchase, for example on labels. This links with protection, since consumers may wish to choose to avoid certain products, ingredients or additives.

Since it is unreasonable to expect individual consumers to make technical decisions on the safety of food foods, Public Health Authorities and official bodies such as the Food and Drugs Administration in the United States or Food Standards Committee in the United Kingdom are necessary to protect consumer interests. With the importance of trade in processed food, international standards such as Codex Alimentarius need to be encouraged. However, there are problems, as noted earlier, on the degree of certainty required before a foodstuff or additive is considered unsafe, and there are "grey areas" in understanding, for example over the interaction of additives and their long term effects. It is important that consumer organisations be active in pressing not only for more research information in this area, but also for more details to be given on product labels as to ingredients and their relative quantities. At least then, if consumers are given as much information as is currently available on the health and safety aspects of foods, their choices are better informed.

REFERENCES

Barker, J.
"Contract Farming", Report, London, HMSO, 1972.

Connor, J. M.
"Food Product Proliferation", A.J.A.E., Vol. 63, No. 4, 1981.

Greig, W. S.
"The Economics of Food Processing", Westport, Avi. 1971.

Handy, C. R. and Padberg, D. I.
"A Model of Competitive Behaviour in the Food Industries", A.J.A.E., Vol. 53, 1971.

Malcolm, J.
"Food and Farming", Conference Paper, Reading University, 1981.

MMC
"Frozen Foodstuffs", Monopolies and Mergers Commission, London, HMSO, 1976.

MMC
"Discounts to Retailers", Monopolies and Mergers Commission, London, HMSO, 1981.

OECD
"Changes in the Processing and Distribution of Milk and Milk Products", Vol. I and II, Paris, 1974.

OECD
"Impact of Multinational Enterprises on National Scientific and Technical Capacities: Food Industry", Paris, 1979.

OECD
"Food Policy", Paris, 1981.

OECD
"Food Margins Analysis: Aims, Methods and Uses", Paris, 1981.

Scherer, F.M.
"The Welfare Economics of Product Variety", J.I.E. Vol. 28, pp. 113-34, 1979.

Papers presented at symposium January 1982.

MANAGING THE DEVELOPMENT OF AGRO-FOOD INDUSTRIES IN RURAL AREAS

by

M. Y. Roucaud
Institut de Développement des Industries
Agricoles et Alimentaires
France

et

M. B. Yon
Institut de Gestion Internationale
Agro-Alimentaire (IGIA)
France

CRITERIA FOR INDUSTRIAL ESTABLISHMENT OF AGRO-FOOD FIRMS IN RURAL AREAS

Authorities nowadays consider that all inhabited rural areas need industrial development because if the local population is to be kept in an area, it has to be provided with a standard of living that is felt to be similar to that in urban areas. This can only be done through the gradual introduction of industry to absorb the surplus labour that agriculture, because of improvements in farm productivity, can no longer utilise.

Agro-food industries are more suited to development in rural areas than other industries for the following reasons: they procure their supplies from the agricultural sector, they work with processes that can often be adopted throughout the sector and they use raw materials available in agricultural areas. The result is a geographical dispersal of firms, which are smaller in size than comparable firms in other industrial sectors. This does not mean that there are no large agro-food groups, but that where such groups do exist, they have numerous industrial plants. These large groups cannot in themselves make up the whole industrial fabric, and the agro-food sector is mainly composed of a considerable number of small and medium sized firms. This pattern of diversification can be seen in all OECD Member countries.

Both the authorities and the entrepreneur have a fundamental role to play in the industrial development of rural areas. The former must create the general environmental conditions that are favourable to such development. The latter has to estimate correctly the chances of launching a viable enterprise. His decision to establish or develop specific projects will be taken in the light of purely industrial criteria which cannot be ignored without risk of failure. Out of this combination of effort can emerge the successful creation and development of new activities.

THE SEARCH FOR COMPARATIVE ADVANTAGE

In general, to survive and develop properly, all firms in the agro-food sector need to be close either to agricultural production centres or to consumption centres. Otherwise the added costs of transport would handicap the firm, particularly in the case of production with a low value-added component. Thus a processing plant situated far from production areas or markets, would be at a considerable disadvantage when compared to its competitors.

Experience has shown that the development of an agro-food industry, and that of the rural area where it is located, seems to require that the rural area has enough available agricultural production or potentially available production to supply the industry. This of course does not prevent the industry from being free to obtain supplies outside the area on occasion, depending on market conditions, nor does it prevent farmers from sending their products to other markets which are temporarily more profitable than that in their own area. However, the existence or potential for an active market or of a large volume of transactions should exist in a rural area if an industry is to choose it for its location.

Location near to production or consumption centres is a matter of some considerable importance. Depending upon the available technology and its cost, some firms, traditionally close to urban consumption centres, have moved nearer to the production areas when it is simpler and more economic to transport the processed products in place of the raw materials. The basic transformation of the agricultural materials, which resembles a "cracking" of these materials, has to be maintained close to the production site because the products obtained are intended for different destinations. Thus, there exists an optimum location for the agro-food firm.

In order to assess the comparative advantage of locating his enterprise in one rural area or another, the entrepreneur examines the quality of the infrastructures (communications, transport, etc.); the cost of real-estate and plant investment, the price of raw materials delivered to the factory, the price of agricultural produce and the cost of delivery to the consumer markets from the factory.

If there is one particularly advantageous factor in a specific rural area, and the other factors are more or less equal, the entrepreneur will locate his firm in the area possessing this comparative advantage. A similar economic calculation will be made by other manufacturers in the same industry who are interested in similar development, until the day comes when industrial concentration in the area is such that it eliminates the comparative advantage, making other areas more attractive for new investment (naturally, on condition that demand for the finished product is still sufficient to warrant the development of production). This selection process, repeated until all comparative advantage has been eliminated, results in regional specialisation.

Those entrepreneurs who establish firms in the neighbouring areas will therefore try to act jointly to secure new conditions as favourable as those prevailing in the better regions. Very probably they will ask the authorities to create better infrastructural facilities, or to give them subsidies to compensate for demonstrable drawbacks. If government intervention is obtained, the result will be to help the area concerned to develop still further, but it will defer the realisation of the potential comparative advantage of neighbouring areas which might otherwise have had an opportunity to develop. It must be emphasized that rural development is accompanied by the specialisation of these areas in certain agricultural products, i.e. those which are transformed by the processing industries.

OBSTACLES TO THE INSTALLATION OF AGRO-FOOD INDUSTRIES IN RURAL AREAS

The obstacles encountered in establishing agro-food industries in rural areas are so numerous, and they assume such different and often unexpected forms, that it is impossible to list them all. They derive mainly from three categories of problems related to: the quality of the infrastructure; resource mobilisation; the rural techno-economic and cultural environment areas still unfamiliar with industrial culture.

i) Quality of infrastructure. Providing newly established firms with adequate physical infrastructure (roads, telecommunications, docks, warehouses, etc.) to meet their needs poses well known problems to decision-makers. But to these must be added problems deriving from the legal or traditional infrastructures in the location areas, (property rights, trade union practices or the general attitude of the rural inhabitants to industry). All these factors can prove disadvantageous to a region, but they can provide the authorities with an occasion to positively balance the comparative advantages of one area in comparison to another.

ii) The mobilisation of resources - first and foremost financing in rural areas is generally considered rather difficult because the risk rating, the returns or the growth are not as good as elsewhere(1). Human resources are also often difficult to assemble in such areas; the available labour is generally insufficiently skilled; the in-migration of skilled labour from similar regions is rare and vocational training facilities are generally insufficient.

iii) Adaptation to the rural techno-economic and cultural environment. New enterprises are sometimes more difficult to establish in rural areas with no industrial tradition. Not only is the available labour force largely unskilled, but the relationships established with the new environment do not correspond to current industrial requirements. When an enterprise is first set up, a "run in" period must be allowed for, and delays must be expected.

1. See the next section.

THE ADVERSE EFFECT OF DISTORTIONS IN THE FINANCIAL MARKET ON SMALL AND MEDIUM FIRMS AND THEIR UNFAVOURABLE IMPACT ON THE DEVELOPMENT OF AGRO-FOOD INDUSTRIES

In rural areas the agro-food sector as a whole, and particularly small firms, suffer from the clear distortion of the capital market which is markedly biased in favour of large companies. A large number of firms in the agro-food sector are family firms which often have insufficient capital to finance their development. These firms are unable to raise capital on the financial market since their stock is not quoted, and they are often too small to interest commercial banks in taking up shares. They have therefore to use their own resources to increase their net worth, a method which is both less rapid and more uncertain than a capital increase through the financial markets.

Where bank loans are concerned the interest rates imposed by the banks on firms are calculated according to the financial risk represented by the client. The difficulty agro-food firms have in accumulating capital increases the risk element, as seen by the banks. The latter are therefore more reluctant to grant loans to small and medium industries than to large enterprises and apply higher interest rates, sometimes amounting to a difference of several points. Therefore the small or medium size firm wishing to invest in a rural area not only takes a risk on its own account, but is also subject to an extra burden when it tries to obtain the capital it needs to function.

An infant industry, moveover, enters the market with a considerable handicap when compared to the market leader, which logically has the lowest cost prices, tends to set the market price and is able to obtain capital more advantageously. Therefore the newly established firm will suffer an adverse effect on its growth and its entrepreneurial capacity will be reduced proportionately.

When there is a question of assessing the creation of a firm, the aforementioned difficulties are carried to extremes, to the point that there is often no investor or lender prepared to finance the firm at the start. Many projects have never seen the light of day because of this serious distortion of the capital market. It is certain that the agro-food sector and rural areas have been more affected by this method of risk evaluation than other industrial sectors, which are generally more profitable and are located in areas which are already developed.

It is very difficult however to make a clear and accurate distinction between the distortions of the capital market and the degree to which a project is unrealistic. This is in fact a measure of the difficulties with which the project will be confronted and is necessarily reflected in the assessment of the overall risk. Thus the interest rate theoretically represents not only the normal return on capital, but is also a reflection of the estimated industrial and financial risks. Only the latter risk is evaluated by the banks, and to the detriment of the small enterprises concerned. If this distinction is made as clear as possible it might enable firms to be treated more fairly; whereas any confusion on the subject could lead to a series of decisions in favour of small and medium firms which might then undertake various projects that are very risky from the industrial point of view.

In order to reduce the banks' perception of the financial risk, firms should be provided with enough equity to reassure the banks and ensure the adequate financing of the development envisaged. This probably requires the creation of financing bodies specialising in agro-food and rural development, so as to be sure that the funds available to these institutions are not invested in other industrial sectors considered less risky and/or more profitable.

Once the industrial firm has been set up, difficult problems arise concerning its continued growth. The agro-food sector is particularly affected by this problem, for during the past 20 years the size of firms and the amount of equipment required have increased considerably and this trend is likely to continue.

When a small firm expands, it necessarily encounters a critical period during its transition from a small to a medium scale enterprise. During the first phase covering the setting up of the firm and its initial development, the determining factors are managerial competence, product quality and marketing. Sales gradually increase but when the moment comes to "take off", the firm must invest heavily, change its technology and methods and acquire new ones. In so doing, it risks its capital (and often its very existence). In this second phase, involving the exponential growth of sales, the limiting factor is the considerable need for capital to cope with the sharp increase in demand.

Steering the enterprise through this critical period raises problems for the head of the firm, who has the choice of growing and succeeding or stagnating until the firm is eliminated. Financing development during the critical phase is difficult, moreover, and if the firm has to call on loan capital, the interest rates will be high because of the overall risk.

Naturally, each time its growth rate accelerates sharply, the firm will encounter the mistrust of the banks (although they are responsive to past successes) and also its own lack of capital, both of which will increase the risks. The same causes produce the same effects, and the interest rates charged reflect the banks' apprehensions with regard to entrepreneurial ventures.

LOCAL, REGIONAL OR NATIONAL AID TO ENCOURAGE THE DEVELOPMENT OF AGRO-FOOD INDUSTRIES IN RURAL AREAS

In order to ensure that an assessment of the comparative advantage of a project will appear positive, the local, regional or national authorities frequently try to grant financial advantages to the firms. The latter must always be treated as a rational individual who compares initial installation expenses with the effective earnings for the time horizon of his investments at the rate of return he would normally expect in the types of industry in which he has experience.

If the industrial project seems feasible, the head of the firm will seek the subsidies and grants to which he is entitled and choose the area (rural perhaps) with an acceptable infrastructure that will bring him the highest amount of aid. A project considered to be non-viable will generally not be launched by a private firm, even if the aid element is high.

Any kind of official aid, in order to have any real influence, must be either considerate at the start or must be spread out over a long period of time; the more underprivileged the rural area, the more this applies. In the case of official aid lasting over a considerable period, however, the entrepreneur will always make a risk assessment, since in the long term government agencies seldom have a continuous line of conduct. This is due to political uncertainties. Moreover, official policy is seldom monolithic. The authorities at each level, whether international, national, regional or local, are intent on carrying out their own development assistance policy, without there necessarily being any co-ordination between them. Often the entrepreneur has a whole range of sources from which he can request aid.

The result of this general attitude is that there is a real "aid market" where each firm tries to place its viable projects. Of course, in the short term, the aid is merely an additional earning which will improve the cash flow during an ensuing period. In the long term, the money required by the authorities to finance investment incentive schemes comes out of taxes. The result of this levy is to reduce all firms' profits and to transfer the product to the area or type of industry or firm which the authorities choose to assist. Because of the slow down in the turnround of funds in the gross margins of successive self-financing operations, and because of management costs and the cost of making studies for industrial projects, it is logical that in the long term incentive schemes cost more to society than they yield.

If the existence of such schemes is to be justified, therefore, some external factor has to have been evaluated favourably by society. In the present case of aid to the installation of agro-food industries, the non-business benefits should be assessed and compared with the final cost of aid operations to the authorities. It seems, however, that this kind of procedure is politically impossible, although it belongs to the welfare economy logic to which the authorities implicitly refer in order to justify their interventions.

READJUSTED DISTRIBUTION OF CAPITAL DUE TO OFFICIAL INTERVENTION

Solutions are difficult to find and seldom wholly satisfactory. Generally, the authorities concentrate on the problem of long-term financing and leave aside the problem of working capital, which is just where firms are treated so unequally by the banks. The authorities are in fact most interested in "investment", which is supposed to improve the employment situation. The problem has been approached in two ways by the authorities: by strengthening firms' own equity; by reduction of capital market distortions.

In order to strengthen the firms' own equity, the authorities can set up institutions specialising in the provision of share capital for small and medium-sized industries, either by creating a considerable part of the capital of these institutions, or by giving them tax concessions or financial advantages when they assist firms; but the authorities should always respect their independence. They provide equity for growing firms for both financial and industrial purposes: a viewpoint which is different from that of the banks.

Furthermore, the authorities may intervene directly in the form of capital-investment financial subsidies, which also strengthen the firm's situation and, therefore, its position as a borrower. These subsidies should be seen as a form of low-cost capital (they should, in fact, be included in the firm's profit and loss account as and when subsidised capital goods are written off, thus being treated as a capital grant made by the authorities for half their amount and as a long-term interest-free loan for the other half)(2).

Original forms of quasi-equity, such as participation loans (halfway between a loan and capital) have been worked out in some countries. The participation loan is in fact a low-priority claim not guaranteed by the firm, in which it resembles capital. However, this claim bears interest, which varies according to the firm's performance, without however falling below or rising above certain stated limits, which are relatively low. The authorities therefore both improve the firm's borrowing status with the banks and reduce the average cost of the capital borrowed.

To counteract the bias of the long-term capital market against small firms, the authorities have been led to intervene directly in the market. They are in fact able to grant loans to firms from public funds at preferential rates (generally much lower than those prevailing on the market). These official loans cover only part of the firm's financing needs, but they enable it to reduce its financing costs. The authorities can also make the institutions specialising in long-term credit responsible for this type of intervention. In that case, the institutions are compensated for the interest lost on the subsidised loans.

In the same way, mutual guarantee societies can increase firms' financial standing and therefore enable them to obtain interest rates that would not be granted if they had no such support.

Tax incentives can either be granted directly to the agro-food firm (accelerated depreciation, over-depreciation, etc.), or indirectly, by granting the lending institution tax exemption on the income from the funds invested (industrial bonds).

The three forms of intervention - increased equity, reduced loan costs and tax incentives - therefore compensate for the shortcomings of the capital market where small firms are concerned.

It should be noted in addition that the authorities are often ill-prepared to make the industrial analysis of projects and the resulting decision to grant aid. Civil servants have neither training nor experience in the management of industrial firms, so they may accept

---

2. In the case of a tax of 50 per cent on enterprise profits.

projects that should have been rejected and reject those that should have been accepted. In either case, non-viable projects will come into being which will probably require permanent assistance. Those that require too high subsidies or are too readily granted are therefore just as hazardous for the future of the economy as insufficient aid. The precise degree of official aid to a firm should be just enough to make the capital market <u>neutral</u> with respect to the size of the firm.

THE BASIS OF DEVELOPMENT: A GOOD USE OF HUMAN RESOURCES

Official intervention alone cannot develop agro-food activities in rural areas. It can, of course, alter the general environmental conditions by creating infrastructures or improving the capital market, but it cannot take the place of people. The problem of manpower, which naturally forms part of the human resources was mentioned earlier. We are referring here to purely entrepreneurial aspects. There have to be people wishing to create firms and make them successful, and they have to have the necessary competence to develop them properly. This point may appear obvious, but it is also fundamental.

The entrepreneur who undertakes a venture is anticipating the future state of the economy. He hopes that the funds invested today will allow him to have an income tomorrow, in such a way that not only will his investment be repaid but there will also be a large enough surplus to ensure future growth. The most difficult part of his undertaking, intellectually speaking, is to evaluate the future of the market. Specifically, will there be a sufficient demand for his products, not only at the start but during the whole life of the firm? The entrepreneur is in fact the person who, having seen, thanks to the information in his possession, that this stable demand will indeed continue to exist, has the courage to launch the venture. Of course, the authorities may guarantee him stable prices and a certain outlet, but in this case he is merely executing their policy, and they will be responsible for the burden of the guarantees provided.

An analysis of economic systems has made it clear that entrepreneurial responsibility, particularly when the investment necessary to start production can be made in a relatively short period of time (a few years at the most), is that which gives the best result for the community in terms of quantities placed at the disposal of the consumer per unit of capital and labour invested. The entrepreneur is the basic factor in initiating and continuing economic development. The success to be achieved depends on the soundness of his assessment of the future and on his determination to succeed. This is what is known as human capital. It can be developed by training, but its qualities can only be expressed under the conditions which have been studied above.

If there are no local or regional entrepreneurs, outside firms with the required enterprise and determination will take their place. Firms should therefore be sought which have already demonstrated these qualities.

It does not seem that the agro-food sector can be developed without recourse to human capital prepared to launch a new industrial venture. The economic context and the conditions in which the installation can be undertaken will be the decisive points in persuading the potential sponsors to launch a project.

An establishment that does not reflect the independent choice of a good businessman is an artificial one. Because of various difficulties in the development of the regions there is sometimes a temptation for the authorities to try to create an agro-food industry on their own initiative, without calling on entrepreneurial partners; for example, through an agricultural co-operative, which can provide a policy excuse for the use of public money for rural development. If, however, the spirit of enterprise and managerial capacity is lacking, a firm that has been created artificially will inevitably run into difficulties and this always leads in the end to the elimination of ill-founded economic activity.

Development in a rural area obeys the same laws as any kind of industrial development. Economic assessments made by a local entrepreneur, by an external firm or by a group of farmers under the influence of the authorities have to be made with the same objectivity, since this is the sole guarantee of the firm's future success.

PERSPECTIVES OF THE FOOD INDUSTRIES AND RELATED GOVERNMENT POLICIES IN THE EIGHTIES

by

Mr. W. Grosskopf
Institute of Agricultural Economics
University of Göttingen
Germany

INTRODUCTION

An analysis of possible developments in the food industries in the 80s involves a synthesis of current knowledge on trends, problems and factors influencing the future supply of and demand for food products. The emerging patterns will help to identify possible areas of concern for policy-makers.

The purpose of this paper is to outline likely long-term changes within the food industry and its environment, insofar as these can be foreseen today. Special attention will be paid to activities within the policy field and to the impact of government actions. Historically, in all OECD countries policy has been important for the agro-food chain, particularly its agricultural sector components. This reflects the economic, political and strategic importance of a sector whose output is a product that satisfies a basic human need.

The following analysis attempts to identify the general lines of potential development within the food industry and its environment. The analysis is neither country nor product specific and is thus cast in rather general terms. Its focus is on the implications for policy in the OECD countries. The ultimate goal of this inquiry is to provide information useful in planning public-policy for the food sector. This sector is important for society and governments because:

- food satisfies a basic human need;

- food is generally a large item in the consumer's budget and is purchased frequently, thus the cost of food is a highly visible element in the cost of living and often has a significant impact on wage negotiations and the cost of labour;
- food is closely associated with health, tradition, ethics and religion;
- food processing plants are often owned by the government itself;
- food plays an important and increasing role in international trade and in foreign policy between the OECD countries as well as in their relations with non-OECD countries.

The following analysis tries to reflect these factors in characterising the broad lines of potential development within the food industry and its environment. Its purpose is to raise issues for discussion rather than provide specific projections or solutions. The paper is divided into two parts. Part one analyses changes which are currently underway in the food industry or are likely to occur in the future. Part two is centred on policy responses to the changes and the possible effects of these responses.

THE IMPACT OF CHANGES IN THE FARM SECTOR

As the food industry is closely connected to the supply of agricultural commodities which provide its basic raw materials, the prices, availabilities and market structures of agricultural commodities are of great significance for the industry.

Most government agricultural programmes in OECD countries involve price rather than direct income support for farmers. In general, in OECD countries plant production (cereals, oilseeds, sugar) and the dairy and beef sectors are most influenced by governmental support programmes; others, particularly the more industrialised, capital intensive pig and poultry sectors are less affected by government support, at least within the domestic market. Food and farm policy tends to be mainly oriented towards the interests of farmers. A variety of policy instruments which differ between commodities and countries focus on the achievement of domestic objectives. One important result is that domestic prices for agricultural commodities differ among OECD countries and from the world price. In most countries domestic prices are above average prices on world markets.

Recent global projections foresee continued world-wide growth in demand for major food commodities in the medium and long term. However, the prospects for continued growth in supply suggest that even with growing demand there will not be an increase in prices in real terms during the eighties. What is likely to continue to be important in domestic and world markets is the variability of prices.

The availability of agricultural commodities could change by the end of the eighties if the production of energy from biomass becomes economic in relation to food production. Currently the economic environment for widespread production of biomass for energy is not commercially competitive. However, if there is continued growth in the real price of oil in the next decade, then this could exert an upward influence on agricultural prices.

Finally, the competitive pressures within the agricultural sector and the agro-food chain are likely to strengthen the rate of growth of farm co-operatives and contract farming. Since agricultural producers are dealing in general with market partners whose size and market power are much greater than their own, it is understandable that farmers, despite their preference for independence, have sought to improve their bargaining position through co-operatives or marketing boards. Contractual agreements between farmers and their market partners are an alternative to the co-operative movement where the bargaining position of farming is stronger. Joint venture contracts, where risks are shared between growers and processors, could be a successful type of organisation in the future but are not yet significant.

CHANGES IN CONSUMER PREFERENCES AND THE GROWTH OF THE CONSUMER MOVEMENT

The combination of slow economic and population growth in the OECD area in conjunction with existing relatively high levels of per capita food consumption imply a slow increase in food demand. However, slow population growth implies a change in the age structure of the population, with consequences for dietary patterns. This demographic development has accentuated the general change of preferences towards a greater awareness of nutritional aspects, the increased consumption of convenience foods, and the greater internationalisation of tastes.

Since basic nutritional requirements are generally met in the OECD countries, the utility of food is increasingly derived from attributes like convenience, nutritional content or image. This situation opens a wide field for advertising and promotion by food processors, which in some countries has led to government measures to control advertising claims that may be contentious or potentially misleading.

It seems likely that the awareness of nutritional aspects will continue to increase even if the growth in real disposable incomes slows down, particularly if the nutritionally preferred food products remain price competitive. Nutritional policy in OECD countries tends to support a greater dietary awareness by consumers.

The growing consumer movement in OECD countries is concerned with a variety of aspects related to food - prices, chemical residues that might be harmful to health, the role of advertising, information regarding the quality and value of foods and the public budgetary support for the agricultural sector. While there continues to be mutual criticism and suspicion between the consumer movement and farmers, food producers and distributors, consumer interests are becoming a more acceptable subject in policy discussions.

CHANGES IN THE FOOD INDUSTRY ITSELF

The food industry has to react to changes outside the sector as well as making its own autonomous adjustments. Two of the latter related to investments and new technologies, and the nature of the competitive process.

In general it is observable that the increasing level of capital investment in the food industry is due to well established trends. In all OECD countries, there is a trend towards higher levels of processing and pre-preparation of foodstuffs. As a result of a continuation of this trend, capital investment could rise considerably in the future. The food industry has less control over its agricultural raw material costs (which are influenced by policy) than over its labour and energy costs. This control is exercised through the efficiency of resource use rather than through the level of wages and other input prices. In most OECD countries wage levels do not always reflect sectoral productivity. There is an incentive to make labour-saving investments. This is also the case with regard to energy and transport use. The process of substitution will probably be enhanced by increasing competition within the food industry and between the sectors of the economy for sales in the context of slower economic growth. The future outlook is thus likely to be one of a lower level of employment in the food industry.

Within the food industry, competition tends to be characterised by rivalry between large companies (e.g. through diversification of the product range, labelling and advertising) and by price competition by the smaller companies. In the case of the former group, the appearance of competition is somewhat of an illusion. It appears that in the future the food industry in the OECD countries will become increasingly divided into parts: a dominant core, consisting of a few large firms producing nationally known brands, and a competitive fringe, which consists of a large number of smaller firms producing less well-known, often regionally-oriented brands, within an environment of strong price competition.

Concentration in the food distribution sector has led to the greater dependence of small food manufacturers on a few distributors. This has resulted in downward pressures on the profit margins of such companies and has further accentuated the tendency towards concentration in the manufacturing sector. In the future it seems likely that the small firms will be complementary to rather than competitive with the major food companies, whilst the larger firms will tend to continue to diversify in the face of sluggish demand.

THE LIMITS OF NATIONAL FOOD MARKETS

The OECD area is the home of multinational food companies. A few of these are completely, or almost completely, specialised in the food sector but some are highly diversified organisations. Their principal contribution remains the transfer of technology and market organisation as well as the effective direction of capital resources. Foreign ownership has been a politically sensitive issue but it seems probable that in the future the beneficial influence of multinationals will be reflected in their improved reception in the countries in which they operate. Nevertheless, much uncertainty still surrounds the future attitudes of host governments with regard to multinationals.

Multinational enterprises operating in the food markets tend to be located in the industries of highest concentration. They are highly capital intensive with high standards in technology and marketing. At least during a period of entry into a new domestic market or of increasing their market share, national food firms in the host country often experience the aggressiveness of the multinational affiliate. The threat of market disturbance from the entry of a multinational is increased if overcapacity is created with its consequent effect upon competitive pressures.

Multinationals usually act more aggressively on domestic markets for two reasons. The first is their ability to exploit their international position in pricing their products. In a given domestic market they can use a "low cost calculation" in determining prices by virtue of internal transfer pricing. To enter into national markets or to increase market share an undercutting price policy may be used. The multinationals experience gained in markets in other countries is helpful in pursuing a successful strategy of expansion. A second aspect of competitive advantage is the edge that multinational enterprises may have over national enterprises in terms of information. Having more and better information on market and price developments, is an important way of creating "power" in markets.

In summary, it is usual that the entry of a multinational into a particular national food market leads first of all to a reduction in prices, followed by industrial concentration and the development of oligopolistic pricing. Considering the dynamic efficiencies created by the competitive process, it is difficult to establish a case for the entry of multinationals into markets dominated by relatively competitive national firms. However, existing trends are likely to continue and multinationals will probably gain an increasing share of food sector markets in the OECD area.

THE INTERNATIONALISATION OF FOOD

It has been evident, particularly since the events of the mid-70s, that domestic food markets are becoming more and more interlinked. The major share of OECD agricultural and food trade is between Member countries (about 70 per cent). About one-third of this trade is in processed food products. It appears that this share will remain relatively stable as it is typical for many countries to employ policies to increase the value added to their domestic agricultural output by escalating the tariffs on processed foods to ensure more domestic processing. In many cases the effective rate of protection for processed food products is high, compared to the rate of protection for unprocessed or lightly-processed products.

On the production side, the agro-food industries within the OECD countries employ similar types of technology. On the consumption side, a convergence of food consumption patterns and preferences appears to be emerging. This internationalisation has been the result of relatively high rates of economic growth, and the declining real cost of the dissemination of producer and consumer information. However, internationalisation has eroded to some extent the local, regional and country-wide advantages in the production of some food products. This raises the potential problem of the spread of a variety of technical and non-tariff barriers to trade, again accentuated by the competitive environment for food demand.

IMPACT OF GOVERNMENTAL ACTIONS AND REACTIONS

During the next decade in most OECD countries the food industry is likely to be confronted by slow growth of demand, continuing technical change and more intensive competition. It will also be required to assimilate major developments, for example those likely to result from the new science of biotechnical engineering and the co-operation with the chemical industry.

These general trends will tend to push the industry in the direction of increasing industrial concentration and product differentiation. On the other hand, some technologies, particularly those linked to computerisation do not necessarily require a large scale of operation to justify their commercial application. Governments will be required to determine their response to these developments. A number of judgements will need to be made as to how and to what extent social control should be exercised over the industry, to what extent technological and economic rationalisation should be influenced in order to maintain desired levels of competition, and to what extent there should be a trade off between consumer protection and consumer freedom. A further question is what role the various components of the food sector (agriculture, processing, distribution, consumers) will play in food policy formation.

The food industry is influenced by government measures relating to overall macro-economic and trade policy, industrial policy and agro-food policy. Given the interdependence between national economies, there is a need to find ways to prevent the policies of one country from adversely affecting others; in the present and future economic environment this will require collective efforts by governments to facilitate and smooth the process of structural change in the economy, both in the agro-food and industrial sectors.

The outlook for the next decade is for slow or even stagnant economic growth in the OECD area. Further, there is a growing awareness of a link between international competition for industrial products and the cost of food. In this environment, a shift away from protectionist agricultural policies in order to foster higher economic growth may be foreseeable. Agricultural product prices may increase at a slower rate than other prices in the economy. This would be reinforced in those cases in which there are problems of over supply of commodities.

Whilst it is foreseeable that in most of the domestic markets of the OECD countries a relatively slow increase in nominal producer prices (decrease in real terms) can be expected, it is nevertheless important to stress that the dangers of protectionist agricultural policies, including non-tariff barriers and changes in regulations could still be a burden for the food industry in the future. Balance of payments problems may tempt countries to increase levels of self-sufficiency in agricultural commodities, but it is to be hoped that the economic situation of the eighties will improve the understanding of the international interdependency between welfare, protection and international trade in agricultural markets.

A common element in industrial policy is the concern with structural change - in promoting industrial growth and efficiency by fostering conditions conducive to free competition - by stimulating the diffusion and application of new technologies, by regulating changes in industrial structures and by protecting the environment.

Competition policy is the traditional field in which governments have attempted to enhance the efficiency of industry. Bearing in mind the tendency towards concentration in the food manufacturing and distribution sectors and the relative bargaining power of the component sectors in the chain (both in purchasing and in selling) government concern with efficient competition is likely to be important during the next decade. However, the advantages of large scale production (and economies of scale) must be weighed against the disadvantages of concentration (and market power). There are links here with technological applications and research and development; whilst the latter is related to the size of the firm, it is not yet clear whether the newer technologies require large sizes of firms in order to be applied economically.

A wide range of environmental protection and food legislation measures are an important part of food industrial policy. The main objectives are the protection of public health and safety and the prevention of fraud. The regulations cover not only the prevention of microbiological and other toxic hazards but also the more difficult control of potential long-term hazards from natural and artificial substances found in food. The complexity in the production and nature of many modern food products has been matched by greater accuracy in the measurement of, for example, chemical constituents and greater scientific knowledge of their effects. However, in many cases the long-term effects are uncertain. This can lead to different reactions by governments.

It may therefore be expected that food regulations - (including packing, storing and labelling regulations) will become more numerous. The implications of this for the food industry are particularly great. Regulations which prohibit or limit a method of food production or particular ingredients affect the cost structure and the relative profitability between products and locations. Some regulations may be used as protectionist measures against imports. In 1979 within the GATT an agreement was reached to reduce these technical barriers through the harmonization of standards. By 1980 over 100 Codex standards had been recommended to governments, but full acceptance of these standards is a slow process.

At this point it must be stressed that trade policies are crucial to the development of the OECD economies. The structural adjustments that are required in response to changes in trade involve radical and often painful changes in many industries. It is understandable that in the short-run protectionist pressures are strong in this situation even if it is accepted that in the long-run greater economic benefits accrue from the exploitation of comparative advantage within a liberal trading framework.

With this perspective in mind, it seems essential that greater harmony in trade policy objectives is necessary. One requirement is that international trade policy bear some relationship to domestic policy. A second requirement is the recognition of the mutual interaction between agricultural and non-agricultural trade, particularly in terms of income and reciprocal effects. A third requirement is the avoidance of trade policies that assume countries may continue to export more than they import. A fourth requirement is that nations accommodate negotiations relating to trade. This latter area includes recognition of implications and costs of adjustment in domestic economies and of the impact on other countries - particularly in terms of price stability - of pursuing domestic policies without regard to worldwide trends.

It seems clear that the open competitive market will not be allowed to exercise full discipline over international trade in food products. It therefore becomes the responsibility of policy-makers to determine the degree and nature of intervention. Multilateral negotiations appear to be the appropriate way to establish the rules of international trade, but there seems to be increasing reluctance to abide by such rules. A further source of uncertainty in this context relates to the use of food trade policy as an aspect of foreign policy. The use of food as an instrument of foreign policy requires a greatly expanded role for governments in international food trade with a consequent unsettling effect on the market. It frequently incurs greater costs on the initiating country than on the target nation in the long-run.

CONCLUSIONS

Even if one were to adopt an optimistic view of the eighties, the range of problems affecting the food industry is likely to become larger and more intensive. Problems have to be overcome in the field of energy and technology, overcapacity, government regulation of domestic markets as well as their impact in the international context. With the growing complexity of the food chain, and the development of increasingly significant horizontal linkages between its component parts and other sectors of the economy, the need for greater coherence in the formulation of policies for the food chain is increasing. Such coherence is necessary in order to ensure that individual measures are effective and is necessary if the relationship between the various agents in the food chain is to be regulated in a manner which is socially acceptable. A major task facing governments during the 1980s will be to achieve a coherent farm and food industry policy.

This paper has raised a number of issues that will concern policy-makers during the next decade. A general observation in the paper is that it is realistic to assume a slowing down of the increase in food demand in OECD countries as a consequence of slower economic and population growth. This will increase the pressure for adjustment in the food industries, affect the bargaining relationships between the component points of the agro-food chain (agriculture, food manufacture, distribution) and potentially increase the pressures for new forms of barriers to trade (technical and non-tariff barriers). At the same time, the application of new forms of technology, the evolution of higher capital-labour ratios and changing consumer preferences are creating a food sector that has a weaker identification with the agricultural sector per se and a greater identification with other branches of industry.

One response to the lengthening agro-food chain and to the interactions of policies has been to examine the concept and practice of "food policy". However, it is not easy to derive a broad and integrated policy given the different structures, problems and interests of the component parts of the chain. While the food industries are obviously interested in the development of agricultural policies, industrial and macro-economic policies are more directly relevant to their interests. Nevertheless, one important aspect that the food policy oncept has highlighted is the necessity for transparency in policy-making - acknowledging and examining the secondary effects of policies and the requirement for more information relevant to the agro-food chain.

Finally, the extent to which perceived problems should be left to the market mechanism or to policy intervention is always a continuing debate in OECD economies. The complexity of modern food products is likely to accentuate this debate both within national economies and with reference to trade policy.

Part III

SHORT SUMMARIES OF THE CONTRIBUTIONS PRESENTED AT THE SYMPOSIUM

I. STRUCTURAL ADJUSTMENTS IN THE FOOD INDUSTRIES

II. CHANGES IN THE RELATIONS BETWEEN FOOD PROCESSING AND AGRICULTURAL PRODUCTION, FOOD DISTRIBUTION AND CONSUMPTION

III. PERSPECTIVES OF THE FOOD INDUSTRIES AND RELATED GOVERNMENT POLICIES IN THE 1980s

I. STRUCTURAL ADJUSTMENTS IN THE FOOD INDUSTRIES

A. PRESENTATION AND DISCUSSION OF NATIONAL CASE STUDIES IN THE FOOD INDUSTRIES

EVOLUTION OF THE FOOD INDUSTRY IN THE EUROPEAN ECONOMIC COMMUNITY

by

J.J. Rateau
Commission of European Communities
Brussels

ECONOMIC IMPORTANCE OF THE INDUSTRIAL FOOD SECTOR(1)

In the EEC

The food industry, which in 1978 produced a turnover of 182,000 million EUA(2), representing 18 per cent of the turnover of all manufacturing industries in the Community, and value added of 35,000 million (10 per cent) employed a workforce of 2,200,000 (9 per cent) and contained 12,900 firms (9 per cent), may be regarded as the largest manufacturing industry in the Community. At national level, it ranks first in Belgium, Denmark, Greece, Ireland, the Netherlands and the United Kingdom, and second in France.

In the primary and secondary processing sectors

The primary and secondary processing sectors are virtually equal in size in terms of their shares (around 10 per cent) of the Community economy as a whole. However, the productivity and added value are higher in the case of secondary processing.

---

1. Cf. the study "the food industry in the EEC" (III/100/81) of February 1981.
2. European Unit of Account.

In the Member States

The German and United Kingdom food industries together account for around 50 per cent of the Community's food industry (60 per cent of its secondary processing sector). France ranks third with 20 per cent, but ranks first in the primary processing sector (25-27 per cent). Italy and the Netherlands together account for 20 per cent of the Community's food industry, although the Netherlands has the better production facilities. Then comes Belgium (4 per cent), Denmark (3 per cent), Ireland, Greece (2 per cent) and Luxembourg (0.1 per cent).

DEVELOPMENT OF THE FOOD INDUSTRY SINCE 1972

The food industry, with a preponderance of small firms, has made, and continues to make, a considerable restructuring effort, particularly in the secondary processing sector.

This led to a 3,900 drop in the number of firms between 1972 and 1978 (23 per cent of the 1972 total), and also to the loss of 188,000 jobs (8 per cent of the 1972 total). Over the same period turnover increased by an average of 18 per cent per annum and value added by 12 per cent.

DEVELOPMENT OF THE EXTERNAL TRADE IN PRODUCTS OF THE FOOD INDUSTRY OF THE EEC AND MEMBER STATES

For the EEC as a whole, trade with third countries in food products(3) continued to increase in 1980; with an increase of 14.5 per cent over 1979 it was in line with the trend shown in recent years, i.e. an average increase of 12 per cent a year from 1974 to 1979. The value of this trade was estimated at 24,400 million EUA; it represented 5.0 per cent of the total trade of the EEC with third countries and for the first time was in surplus to the extent of 1,800 million EUA.

Foreign trade of Member States: the foreign trade of Member States includes intra-Community trade. Taking this into account, the main trading partners are Germany, France, the Netherlands and the United Kingdom.

---

3. Unprocessed agricultural products excluded.

Germany, the largest importer and third largest exporter, has an overall deficit of 2,000 million EUA in 1979; whereas France, the largest exporter and third largest importer, has a trade surplus of 2,100 million EUA. The Netherlands, the second largest exporter and fourth largest importer is the second largest beneficiary of trade in food products, with a surplus of 1,700 million EUA. The United Kingdom - the second largest importer and fourth largest exporter - has the largest trade deficit in the Community (2,600 million EUA).

Foreign trade of food products

The main products traded are beverages and dairy products, representing 47 per cent of exports, while animal feed, oils and fats and chocolate products account for 53 per cent of imports.

Development of the EEC's external trade since 1974

Trade in food products with non-Member countries has expanded steadily in recent years, reaching an annual growth rate of 14.5 per cent for exports and 10.1 per cent for imports since 1974. In relation to the Community's external trade overall, food products account for 5.3 per cent of total exports and 5.9 per cent of total imports. In other respects, if we follow the practice adopted in some Member States of excluding animal feed and tobacco, the food industry produced an aggregate surplus of 10,000 million EUA from 1974 to 1980.

PROSPECTS FOR GROWTH IN THE INDUSTRIAL FOOD SECTOR

The factors governing the development of the food industry can be divided into three groups. The first relates to demand, i.e the numbers requiring food and the type of foodstuffs which these individuals wish, or are able to obtain. The second group concerns supply, which, in addition to natural hazards, is subject to technical, economic and even political constraints. The third group relates to scientific and technical progress, which will enable undertakings to adapt the essential elements of their production process to the requirements of the populations concerned and to face the challenge of competition.

Although inadequate, the Community has considerable scientific potential(4) with which to meet the requirements of the food industry. The Community has in 1979 over 400 research laboratories employing 5,000 graduates. Yet the estimated budget of 250 million EUA allocated to this work represents only 0.1 per cent of the industry's turnover. This low percentage has fallen since 1973 when it was estimated at 0.3 per cent.

As regards supplies, the essentially agricultural origin of the raw materials employed entails numerous disadvantages and constraints, for example the variable quality and quantity of seasonal produce, and high prices. Nevertheless, the existence of a powerful, modern agricultural industry represents, and will continue to constitute, a growing opportunity for the foodstuffs industry which, as a result, will be partially shielded from the fluctuations affecting agricultural production and supplies on a world scale.

Consequently, demand will be the decisive factor affecting the future of the EEC food industry.

Development of domestic demand: in 1982, the Community of Ten represents a market of 270 million people which, with high living standards and a high degree of urban concentration, offers excellent opportunities for the food industry. However, the low rate of increase in the population and hence in aggregate purchasing power, together with better education in dietary matters, is likely to stabilize domestic demand in volume terms. This situation favours dynamic firms which are strong on innovation and competition, but will mean restructuring and a loss of jobs for the industry as a whole.

Exports: the dynamism of undertakings is the driving force behind exports. Nevertheless, international competition does not always allow the most eager Community firms to export because of the advantages which their foreign competitors enjoy in this field. Refunds are the main form of aid available to the Community foodstuffs exporter and these frequently prove inadequate.

Since an increase in these refunds could hardly be contemplated, particularly in view of the financial implications of such a step, it would be desirable to be able to employ other measures which would help our exporters to compete with their foreign counterparts.

---

4. Cf. "Directory of Industrial Food Research Centres" (1980) EUR 6692.

The request of the Third World: the anticipated increase in the world's population from 4,500 million at present to 6,000 million in the year 2,000 is the major problem of the future for the international community. The food industry worldwide and, more particularly, in the Third World will have a key role to play: clearly the Community industry can make a major contribution to solving this problem. Expansion of the Third World's food industry will require scientific, technological, financial and organisational resources which are far beyond the reach of these countries at present and must therefore be supplied by the industrialised nations. But in a free enterprise system industrial co-operation cannot be made mandatory and must be allowed to develop in a climate of mutual trust with full respect for the legitimate interests of all concerned.

CONCLUSIONS

Over the next ten years, the food industry in the industrialised countries is likely to follow the same pattern as in the last ten years, when it was marked by a low increase in overall output, high technological development which led to a fall in the labour force and the restructuring of firms. Prospects for growth will therefore be based on an expansion of exports to developed countries, on success in penetrating new markets, and above all on a higher level of food production and consumption in the Third World.

The fact that investors are now seeking to diversify into the food sector bears witness to its new interest as a growth area in Europe and worldwide.

STRUCTURAL ADJUSTMENT IN THE CANADIAN FOOD AND BEVERAGE SECTOR

by

Mr. P.K. Gorecki
Economic Council of Canada

The paper examines selected aspects of the structure (concentration, trade and tariffs, foreign ownership), conduct (pricing policy, advertising and product promotion, foreign vs. domestic firm conduct), and performance (prices, profitability, productivity), of the Canadian food and beverage sector in the 1970s. The major findings can be summarised as follows:

- The 18 individual industries which comprise the food and beverage sector, vary considerably in their relative importance. For example, in 1978, Slaughtering and Meat Processors accounted for 25.1 per cent of sector shipments, followed by Dairy Products (15.5 per cent) with Wineries (0.5 per cent) ranked last.

- Most food and beverage sector industries fell into the slightly to moderately concentrated oligopoly category, suggesting that the sector is, by and large, workably competitive.

- Over the period 1970 to 1978 there appeared to be a centripetal pattern of change in industry concentration.

- Poultry Processors and Dairy Products saw changes during the 1960s and 1970s in the market structure of their major agricultural inputs. Legally mandated producer cartels, with power to raise prices and restrict output, were established for industrial or manufactured milk, chickens and turkeys.

- The food and beverage sector, although experiencing tariff reductions because of the Kennedy Round, had nevertheless an effective tariff rate that substantially exceeded that for manufacturing. In some instances, particularly Dairy Products, Breweries and Wineries, this was supplemented by non-tariff barriers.

- International trade is generally unimportant in the food and beverage sector compared with manufacturing, although there are some prominent exceptions, including Fish Products (74 per cent of domestic shipments exported in 1978) and Wineries (56 per cent of domestic consumption imported in 1978).

- Foreign owned firms account for a much smaller proportion (one third) of food and beverage sector shipments than for manufacturing (one half). The incidence of foreign ownership, however, is highly uneven, within the sector, varying, in 1978 from 13.5 per cent of shipments in Slaughtering and Meat Processors to 71.0 per cent for Miscellaneous Food Processors NES. Over the period 1970 to 1976 a number of substantial shifts in the importance of foreign ownership occurred.

- In the late 1970s and 1980s the successful advent of generic and no-name grocery products threatens to alter the relative bargaining power between the retailer and food processor in favour of the former.

- The large increase in food prices in the 1970s was not due to the exercise of monopolistic power by the food and beverage sector, but rather developments outside the sector.

- Food and beverage sector industry profits were not, by and large, persistently high or low - evidence of adverse performance.

- Labour productivity in the Canadian food and beverage sector lags considerably behind that of the United States, the benchmark used for evaluation purposes (probably reflecting such factors as small market size and short growing season).

- Radical change in public policy toward the food and beverage sector is not called for on the basis of the evidence presented in this paper.

Table 1

CONCENTRATION IN THE FOOD AND BEVERAGE SECTOR: 1970-1978

	Industry	Concentration(a)				Number			
		Firms		Establishments		Firms		Establishments	
SIC Code	Title	1970	1978	1970	1978	1970	1978	1970	1978
1011	Slaughtering & Meat Processors	53.4	44.0	20.8(b)	17.9(b)	407	440	453	491
1012	Poultry Processors	37.0	39.2	21.9	19.4	86	69	102	87
102	Fish Products	39.1	46.3	14.3	17.4	252	263	344	347
1031	Fruit & Vegetable Canners & Preservers	41.6	39.0	27.4	26.8	187	153	238	197
1032	Frozen Fruit & Vegetable Processors	n.a.	58.5	n.a.	46.6(b)	34	29	34	35
104	Dairy Products	29.2	34.7	12.9	16.7	643	317	880	485
105	Flour & Breakfast Cereal Products	70.0	64.7	38.1	33.1	32	30	51	49
106	Feed Industry	29.4	28.0	10.3(b)	10.1	647	472	789	593
1071	Biscuit Manufacturers	68.0	73.0	44.6	47.4	34	25	42	35
1072	Bakeries	31.4	32.4	12.5	14.7	1857	1377	1921	1440
1081	Confectionery Manufacturers	52.7	48.0	39.4	40.9(b)	132	96	139	106
1082	Cane & Beet Sugar Processors	80-100(c)	75.8	68.8(b)	n.a.	7	9	14	15
1083	Vegetable Oil Mills	78.4	76.1	78.4	n.a.	10	8	10	10
1089	Miscellaneous Food Processors NES	33.6	35.5	22.4	22.0	228	228	275	286
1091	Soft Drink Manufacturers	45.7	48.2	18.1	14.7	333	203	395	255
1092	Distilleries	86.4	79.1	55.0(b)	45.6(b)	12	17	27	34
1093	Breweries	94.0	98.9	41.6	43.0	9	8	42	41
1094	Wineries	64.1	76.4	53.3	42.2	14	17	22	29
	Average	55.5	55.4(d)	34.1(e)	28.7(e)	274	209	321	252

a. Since establishments and firms were ranked by shipments concentration is estimated as the percentage of industry shipments accounted for by the largest four firms or establishments.

b. The data source publishes only the eight establishment concentration ratio. It was assumed that the leading four establishments were twice as large as the next four.

c. Author's estimate, based on establishment concentration ratio and the fact that the leading four firms accounted for 11 of the industries' 14 establishments.

d. If 1032 is excluded then the average falls to 55.3.

e. If the average is estimated only for industries for which data is available for both years then 34.1 becomes 28.8 and 28.7, 27.5.

n.a. Not available for reasons of confidentiality.

Source: Statistics Canada, Industrial Organisation and Concentration in the Manufacturing Mining and Logging Industries, Cat. ≠ 31-402, various issues and information provided by the Manufacturing and Primary Industries Division, Statistics Canada.

Table 2

TRADE AND TARIFFS IN THE FOOD AND BEVERAGE SECTOR: 1966-1978

SIC Code	Industry Title	Import Penetration(a)			Export Orientation(b)			Tariffs(c)			
								Nominal		Effective	
		1966	1970	1978	1966	1970	1978	1966	1970	1966	1970
1011	Slaughtering and Meat Processors	5.6	6.5	7.6	7.7	7.7	9.1	4.21	4.72	6.45	9.76
1012	Poultry Processors	1.2	0.8	3.4	0.4	0.4	0.3	12.14	11.60	42.65	40.37
102	Fish Products	19.0	26.2	42.8	55.0	57.5	74.2	12.66	8.07	34.29	23.25
1031	Fruit & Vegetable Canners & Preservers	19.1	19.7	28.3	6.9	7.5	7.8	13.89	12.12	24.38	20.49
1032	Frozen Fruit & Vegetable Processors							n.a.	n.a.	n.a.	n.a.
104	Dairy Products	1.7	1.6	2.3	3.1	3.8	2.7	12.56(d)	14.02(d)	44.65(d)	49.13(d)
105	Flour & Breakfast Cereal Products	2.2	2.5	3.9	30.8	26.1	30.7	1.82/15.89(e)	0.95/14.32(e)	6.36/30.04(e)	-1.37/26.49(e)
106	Feed Industry	0.6	1.2	1.6	3.7	3.9	4.4	8.02	6.37	22.58	16.78
1071	Biscuit Manufacturers	5.5	5.4	6.5	4.2	8.3	6.8	7.98	5.52	9.26	4.47
1072	Bakeries	0.8	0.8	1.9	0.8	0.8	1.7	14.85	8.83	23.99	13.06
1081	Confectionery Manufacturers	11.5	13.5	20.3	3.0	4.9	4.7	12.99	11.08	20.09	15.38
1082	Cane & Beet Sugar Processors	4.3	2.4	3.3	1.6	1.1	10.8	14.55	11.50	37.35	29.49
1083	Vegetable Oil Mills	43.3	39.2	34.2	26.5	23.4	22.6	3.18	1.99	35.19	19.56
1089	Miscellaneous Food Processors, NES	7.6	8.4	12.8	4.7	3.3	3.9	8.86	5.61	19.31	9.95
1091	Soft Drink Manufacturers	1.0	0.7	1.1	0.0	0.2	0.3	6.86	3.30	7.32	0.41
1092	Distilleries	17.2	16.8	25.1	48.6	53.8	46.0	n.a.	n.a.	n.a.	n.a.
1093	Breweries	0.4	0.5	2.9	2.6	2.6	5.5	n.a.	n.a.	n.a.	n.a.
1094	Wineries	42.4	39.8	56.2	0.3	0.4	0.9	n.a.	n.a.	n.a.	n.a.
	Food & Beverage Sector	6.6	7.0	10.4	9.6	9.7	11.6	9.20(f)	7.96(f)	23.20(f)	19.04(f)
	Manufacturing	21.0	25.5	31.6	18.8	26.2	30.4	12.40(g)	10.76(g)	20.11(g)	16.88(g)

a. Imports/(Domestic Shipments - Exports + Imports). The denominator is sometimes referred to as domestic disappearance.

b. Exports/Domestic Shipments.

c. The industry SIC used for tariffs does not match exactly, in all cases, that used for import penetration and export orientation. See footnotes d and e below.

d. These tariff rates are for dairy factories which appears to be the same as 104, Dairy Products, except that process cheese manufacturers is excluded.

e. The first tariff rate, in each pair, is for Flour Mills, the second Breakfast Cereal Manufacturers.

f. Excludes 1092, 1093 and 1094.

g. Simple average of two-digit industry rates in Manufacturing Sector.

n.a. = Not available from data sources.

Source: Department of Industry, Trade and Commerce, Manufacturing Trade and Measures 1966-1980. (Ottawa: Department of Industry, Trade and Commerce, 1981) and B.W. Wilkinson and K. Norrie, Effective Protection and the Rate of Return to Capital. (Ottawa: Information Canada, 1975), Table 3-1, pp. 27-31, Table 3-4, pp. 42-43, Table A-1, pp. 76-80, Table A-2, pp. 81-82.

Table 3

THE IMPORTANCE OF FOREIGN OWNERSHIP IN THE FOOD AND BEVERAGE SECTOR: 1970-1976

SIC Code	Industry Title	Percentage of Shipments Accounted for by				Percentage of Establishments Accounted for by			
		U.S. Firms		All Foreign Firms		U.S. Firms		All Foreign Firms	
		1970	1976	1970	1976	1970	1976	1970	1976
1011	Slaughtering & Meat Processors	n.a.	11.3	13.8	13.5	n.a.	3.6	4.2	4.8
1012	Poultry Processors	12.0	18.1	12.0	18.1	7.8	13.7	7.8	13.7
102	Fish Products	n.a.	15.2	33.1	16.1	n.a.	8.1	16.9	9.3
1031	Fruit & Vegetable Canners & Preservers	n.a.	53.8	64.0	64.6	n.a.	19.1	24.4	25.9
1032	Frozen Fruit & Vegetable Processors	29.7	45.9	29.7	45.9	17.6	35.1	17.6	35.1
104	Dairy Products	26.7	29.2	29.9	31.3	7.4	10.9	8.8	11.7
105	Flour & Breakfast Cereal Products	n.a.	63.0	48.2	63.0	n.a.	34.8	23.5	34.8
106	Feed Industry	n.a.	n.a.	19.4	24.4	n.a.	n.a.	4.2	8.4
1071	Biscuit Manufacturers	n.a.	n.a.	71.8	52.2	n.a.	n.a.	31.0	19.4
1072	Bakeries	n.a.	n.a.	21.7	21.7	n.a.	n.a.	1.7	1.9
1081	Confectionery Manufacturers	40.1	32.1	79.2	65.7	12.2	17.0	18.0	26.5
1082	Cane & Beet Sugar Processors	n.a.	n.a.	n.a.	n.a.	n.a.	n.a.	n.a.	n.a.
1083	Vegetable Oil Mills Processors	n.a.	n.a.	n.a.	n.a.	n.a.	n.a.	n.a.	n.a.
1089	Miscellaneous Food Processors NES	52.7	51.6	72.0	71.0	25.8	26.2	33.5	34.1
1091	Soft Drink Manufacturers	n.a.	n.a.	50.9	54.0	n.a.	n.a.	11.9	15.7
1092	Distilleries	n.a.	n.a.	n.a.	30.6	n.a.	n.a.	n.a.	46.6
1093	Breweries	n.a.	n.a.	n.a.	n.a.	n.a.	n.a.	n.a.	n.a.
1094	Wineries	n.a.	n.a.	n.a.	36.2	n.a.	n.a.	n.a.	24.9
	Food & Beverage Sector	24.3	27.2	33.2	33.9	6.4	8.7	8.8	10.8
	Manufacturing	41.9	41.0	51.9	50.9	9.1	10.2	11.9	13.3

n.a. Not available for reasons of confidentiality.

Source: Statistics Canada, Domestic and Foreign Control of Manufacturing, Mining and Logging Establishments in Canada, Cat. ≠ 31-401, various issues.

STRUCTURAL ADJUSTMENT IN THE AGRICULTURAL AND FOOD INDUSTRIES IN FRANCE DURING THE PAST TWENTY YEARS

by

Mr. B. Ewenczyk
Bureau de l'Economie Générale
Ministry of Agriculture
France

The agricultural and food industries sector now accounts for over 10 per cent of industrial employment, has a large trade surplus and, due to its geography, is an essential element in the French industrial fabric. This continually changing sector is made up of very different sized units whose dynamism depend on diverse factors.

A SIGNIFICANT CHANGE IN LIFE STYLES AND A LARGE INCREASE IN PURCHASING POWER HAVE RESULTED IN A NEW CONSUMPTION PATTERN

In 20 years the ambient variables have changed in kind as a result of urbanisation, the decline of the rural population, the development of female labour, the reduction in working hours, and the lower rate of population growth. At the same time purchasing power has considerably increased so that on the whole, while the place of food consumption has suffered a relative decline, falling from 36 per cent of consumer expenditure in 1959 to 22 per cent in 1980, within that consumption the share of the agricultural and food industries has grown from 72 per cent to 78 per cent of the total.

OPENING UP OF MARKETS

This involves a process of unification of the national market through the concentration of distribution and the development of mass-market branded products. It also involves the internationalisation of the economy, the percentage of foreign trade involved having increased from 5 per cent to 12 or 13 per cent over the period examined. France's share in the world market for agro-food products increased from 7.3 per cent to 10.3 per cent between 1961 and 1978 in the case of meat and dairy products and from 5.5 per cent to 8 per cent in the case of the remaining products.

THE PRODUCTION SYSTEM HAS BEEN STRONGLY RESTRUCTURED AND FORMS A COMPOSITE WHOLE OF VARYING PERFORMANCE

The agricultural and food industries constitute a young industrial sector still strongly marked by its scattered origin, with the regional markets close to the agricultural producers upstream. The sector on the whole has become concentrated and given rise to some nationwide undertakings. At present 3 per cent of firms are responsible for 40 per cent of turnover and 10 per cent for 60 per cent; between 1969 and 1975 the number of firms declined by almost 40 per cent. From the early 1960s and particularly since 1967-1968 a restructuring has taken place in the agro-food industries. In the first phase there was a regrouping of firms in the sector, which resulted in the formation of private or co-operative groupings of significant size. The second stage began in 1973 and featured an inflow of external capital to the agro-food industry sector (industrial groups and state capital combined). In 1980 some 50 firms had over a thousand permanent staff. There was increasing penetration of foreign capital in the early 1960s, and a second phase 10 years later involving particularly British capital, and lastly, since 1978, North American capital. This penetration has occurred in secondary processing with certain special product lines strongly dominated by firms controlled by foreign capital. Conversely, French firms have only much more recently started to invest elsewhere in the world, but despite their considerable lag in this field they are now making mainly commercial investments chiefly oriented towards bordering countries and the United States.

At present the agro-food industry sector is therefore composed of a few dynamic firms, together with a family-type sector which is still considerable in areas close to distribution, and a large number of medium and small firms particularly in the primary processing sector. These medium and small firms produce select products, but their future is problematical because of the economic crisis.

Will the agro-food industries be able to face up to the new challenges? World competition is increasing and many strategic issues are involved.

STRUCTURAL ADJUSTMENT IN THE FOOD INDUSTRIES OF THE FEDERAL REPUBLIC OF GERMANY

by

Mr. Werner Grosskopf
Institute of Agricultural Economics
University of Göttingen
Germany

Over the last 30 years the part of the food system, interposed between farmers and consumers, has been subject to a variety of pressures making for continuing and often radical change in the structure and grouping of organisations.

Expenditures on food continue to account for a large part of the consumer budget, almost one-fifth of total consumer expenditure. The development of the shares has been as follows:

Food spending as a per cent of disposable income		Shares of this going to		
		Agricultural Production	Food Industries	Food Distribution
Year		Per cent		
1960	37.3	52	36	12
1970	30.4	48	41	11
1980	20.1	46	44	10

Food prices at the consumer level have demonstrated a rising trend and have made a major contribution to the average inflation rate of the last ten years. The "restrictive" price policy of the EEC since 1977 could be one reason but changes in productivity and in the degree of competition within the total food sector seem to be the main basis of these price trends.

By the beginning of the 1960s, Germany had a relatively unconcentrated food sector. But concentration has increased markedly within the last fifteen years. Still today, however, one finds large stock companies in the neighbourhood of small family-oriented firms within the food sector.

The following figure gives an overview of the size structure of the German food industry. More than 90 per cent are so-called small sized or middle classed enterprises.

SIZE DISTRIBUTION OF FOOD PROCESSING ENTERPRISES
(Ranked by the numbers of employees)

Employees per firm	1970		1977		1979		1985(1)
	No.	%	No.	%	No.	%	%
1 - 19	5779	(60.0)	722	(14.4)	621	(12.8)	50.6
20 - 99	2580	(27.0)	3148	(62.8)	3082	(63.4)	
100 - 299	941	(3.5)	843	(16.8)	855	(17.6)	47.4
300 - 999	416	(4.3)	264	(5.3)	260	(5.4)	
1000 and more	46	(0.5)	39	(0.8)	40	(0.8)	2.0
Total	9552	(100.0)	5016	(100.0)	4858	(100.0)	100.0

1. Projected.

The most significant growth of concentration has occurred in those product groups characterised by high advertising expenditures. For these products the expertise of firms lies in creating new product variations, advertising and promoting them, and using field sales personnel to see that their products receive favourable treatment on the grocer's shelf. Examples are the tobacco, the ice cream and frozen food industry, the soup processing industry and the margarine and infant food industry. In these sectors only a few, sometimes only one to three companies, act as market and price leaders having a high market share.

Summarising, the food processing industries can be divided into two parts: a dominant core, which consists of a few very large firms producing nationwide brands, and accounting for a significant share of industry sales; and a competitive fringe, which consists of a large number of smaller firms producing less well-known, often regionally oriented brands.

During the past decade, the food industry has been very much at the forefront of the merger movement, and the effect on the basic structure of the industry can be seen from the fact that today the top twenty firms in the industry account for nearly 35 per cent of the industry's sales (excluding animal feedstuffs). This would seem to be a very conservative measurement of the degree of concentration, which does not include sales outside the food sector.

In different markets and within different groups of the same food market the instruments of competition are varied. Very small enterprises may exploit local or regional situations, producing specialities and acting like a monopolist. The middle-sized firms normally have to accept a strong price competition. And the large companies use all possibilities of non-price competition. In the case of the development of convenience foods, with large firms opened and widened the markets via advertising and labelling, estimates of advertising costs show quite clearly that during the last ten years expenditure increased tremendously. As a percentage of the total sales for 1970 the estimates were for a maximum of 1.8 per cent. Today this ratio is calculated on 3.0 per cent for the whole food industry.

Traditionally, food exports by the German food industry are low compared to total production. But in connection with the open food market in the EC, particularly since the enlargement and the membership of the United Kingdom, the export share of production going for export has been increasing.

Beginning in the mid 1950s Germany became an attractive investment location for foreign-based multinational corporations. Today Germany is, without doubt, an important market for foreign-owned food firms. Half of the firms ranked among the 20 largest firms (based on sales) are foreign-owned. Some of the more dynamic markets are dominated by these firms. Their legal form is normally that of a stock company. In comparison, the investment activities of German firms are mainly domestically oriented.

In terms of legislation, the food industries are generally treated on a par with the other sectors of the economy. But there are some sector-specific regulations regarding advertising and nutritional policy. For example, TV-advertising for tobacco products is limited. Health policy tries to ensure that foods do not pose a health risk, therefore relatively strong regulations for the conditions of manufacturing, storaging and transportation of the products are specified. There are also some special regulations concerning substitutes for dairy products, meat analogs and synthetic sweeteners. The possible ingredients of fruit juices are regulated and a special order governs the quality of beer.

In the longer-run existing trends in the food sector may be leading to a decline of competition. In most cases the changes under way in structure are tending to re-inforce the market power of the few leading firms. Farmer organisations may be able to protect themselves through countervailing actions. Consumers are lacking in this potential power. In the light of this changes in food policy may be required.

ASPECTS OF FOOD INDUSTRIES IN THE NETHERLANDS: STRUCTURE AND GOVERNMENT POLICY

by

Mr. E. Klein
Ministry of Agriculture and Fisheries
The Hague

IMPORTANCE OF THE FOOD INDUSTRIES(1)

The food industries are an important industrial component in the Netherlands. They provide about 16 per cent of industrial employment (or 3.5 per cent of total employment, i.e. 160,000 persons), about 25 per cent of industrial turnover, 15 per cent of industrial added value (or 3.5 per cent of NNP)(2), 17 per cent of industrial exports and 20 per cent of industrial investments. Since 1960 the share of the food industries in total industrial activity has remained virtually unchanged.

Domestic farmers provide the major part of the agricultural raw materials processed by the food industries. Food manufacturing purchases over 60 per cent of total farm output. Mainly due to the strong expansion of horticulture (vegetables and ornamental products) this proportion has not changed during the last two decades. The mutual close involvement is also apparent from the shipments of the food industry to Dutch agriculture: about 27 per cent of home sales, mainly animal feeds.

TRENDS IN INDUSTRY STRUCTURE

During the period 1971-1981, the food processing industry has concentrated its production in fewer firms at a rate faster than the whole of manufacturing industry.

---

1. In this paper "food industries" includes all manufacturers of food and beverages.
2. Net national product.

Excluding the smallest firms - up to 10 employees - it seems that, as for employment and sales, medium-sized firms have lost some ground, while the big firms have increased their market share.

Some sectors of the food industry are highly concentrated. In flour, sugar and beer a small number of firms provide 75 per cent or more of the turnover of the sector, while in dairy the four firm concentration ratio is tending to 80 per cent. Most firms restrict their activities to one sector of the food industry. However, a few large concerns do business in various sectors.

In some sectors, the supply of local raw materials strongly determines the level of production, e.g. dairy, sugar and potato starch. Therefore it is not surprising that especially in these sectors the market share of co-operatives is considerable. Since 1958 the market share of co-ops increased slightly to about 35 per cent in 1980.

The presence of foreign ownership is small in sectors which primarily purchase their raw materials from or sell their products directly to Dutch farmers (e.g. dairy, sugar, animal feeds and slaughterhouses). On the other hand, foreign subsidiaries or majority participation is much more significant in sectors which do not have close ties to Dutch farmers or are heavily dependent on imported farm products (e.g. meat products, cakes/biscuit, cocoa, coffee and tea). Provisional data indicate that during the period 1971-1978 the number of foreign-controlled food firms tripled. Since 1971, the market share of these foreign owned firms has approximately doubled to about 10 per cent in 1978.

PERFORMANCE

During 1960-1980 the volume of production by the food industries doubled, i.e. it grew at an average annual rate of about 3.5 per cent. During the last decade the sectors dairy, slaughterhouses (excluding poultry), animal feeds, fish, food potato products and beer grew substantially. Sectors producing flour, bread, biscuits, cocoa, confectionary and preserved fruits and vegetables grew relatively slowly or not at all (see tables 1 and 2).

During 1960-1980 the volume of exports grew at an average annual rate of about 7.0 per cent while the volume of domestic deliveries grew much slower. In addition to the formation of the Common Market, a difference between the product of exports and domestic demand explains these different growth rates. In domestic deliveries the category "other food stuffs", for which demand rose slowly, have the biggest market share. On the other hand, animal products, for which demand is still rising, account for over 50 per cent of exports. These developments imply an increasing dependence of the food industries on exports (over 50 per cent in 1980).

Table 1

QUANTITY INDICES

	1960	1970	1980
Animal products	100	147	193
Other food products	100	138	180
Beverages	100	254	425
Tobacco	100	145	176
Total	100	151	200

Source: Central Bureau of Statistics

Throughout the period 1960-1980 capital investment remained at a high level. Despite production increases employment decreased; labour productivity rose at an average annual rate of nearly 5 per cent. Profitability has declined as in all manufacturing.

GOVERNMENT POLICY

Besides macro-economic policy and the Common Agricultural Policy, Government policy in respect of the food industries is mainly incorporated in general Government policy in relation to industry. Until the early seventies, Dutch industry developed quite smoothly. Government policy was mainly aimed at improving infrastructure and at mitigating wage-increases. In the seventies Dutch industry suffered from the world economic recession. In this period firms in financial difficulties were aided through individual aid operations: the so-called defensive approach. In the late seventies however, the increasing number of firms receiving aid generated a belief that competitive distortions were being created and that structural problems were emerging. From 1979 onwards the defensive approach was abandoned and the aid to individual firms was gradually eliminated. The policy gradually developed into a more offensive and anticipative approach, aimed at improving and strengthening the competitive position of sectors and industrial processes with medium-term viability and stimulating adjustments and innovations in industry.

During the late sixties and the early seventies substantial problems arose in several sectors of the food industries. As a result structural examinations and/or reorganisations took place in malt (1972-1974), (Dutch) crispbakes (1974), and poultry (1976-1979). These measures were taken in consultation with employers, employees and the Government; these consultations were mostly formalised in special committees.

Nearly all the above mentioned measures fall in the category of the "defensive" approach. However, the change in the Government's industrial policy towards positive adjustment and an anticipative approach has also been adopted in respect of food industries. Development credits have been granted to numerous projects in various sectors. Additionally, within the framework of the Governmental energy policy, careful sector examinations of the possibilities and desirabilities of energy saving are being made in the sectors dairy, bakeries and compound feed, while some other branches are considering similar examinations.

Table 2

MAIN DATA FOR THE FOOD INDUSTRIES(1) 1972 AND 1979

	Employment		Production value		Census added value(2)	Gross added value
	1972 (thousands)	1979 (thousands)	1972 (f million)	1979 (f million)	1972 (f million)	1979 (f million)
Dairy	24.6	22.0*	6,813	9,600*	1,119	1,250*
Meat (products)(3)	25.3	22.8	4,661	8,143	837	1,144
Fish	1.2	1.3*	98	220*	37	50*
Flour, groats - rice hulling	2.1	1.9	733	1,167	133	180
Sugar	5.0	4.5	719	1,283	225	345*
Margarine, fats, oils	5.1	4.4	1,719	3,631	400	348
Preserved fruits and vegetables	10.9	7.9	1,138	1,567	461	388
Bread, biscuits, cakes	25.7	21.6	1,271	2,189	617	866
Cocoa, chocolates, confectionery	11.9	8.6	1,119	2,422	409	462
Animal feeds	15.2	11.3	3,769	7,556	686	828
Other food stuffs	17.3	16.0	2,304	4,518	804	979
Alcohol, distilleries	2.4	1.9	260*	515	140*	151
Beer, malt	7.4	7.6	723	1,684	533	710
Soft drinks	4.2	2.8	435	755	239	185
Total	158.3	134.6	25,760	45,250*	6,640	7,886*

1. Data referring to activity units with 10 or more persons employed.
2. "Census added value" = gross added value + certain costs (rent, insurance, travelling, mail, telephone, advertising, etc.).
3. Excluding abattoirs.
* Estimate by Ministry of Agriculture and Fisheries.
Source: Central Bureau of Statistics.

STRUCTURAL ADJUSTMENT IN THE UNITED KINGDOM FOOD MANUFACTURING INDUSTRY OVER THE PAST TWENTY YEARS(1)

by

B. G. A. Watts
Ministry of Agriculture, Fisheries and Food
United Kingdom

INTRODUCTION

The food manufacturing industry plays an important part in the economy of the United Kingdom. It contributes some 2-2½ per cent of GDP and some 8 per cent of the value added of manufacturing industry; it employs some half a million people. Like the rest of the economy, it has undergone considerable change during the last twenty years.

STRUCTURE OF THE FOOD INDUSTRY

The United Kingdom food manufacturing industry is highly concentrated and the level of concentration is slightly greater than the average for all manufacturing industry. Over the period 1958 to 1973, the average five-firm industry concentration ratio for food manufacturing, defined in terms of employment, rose from 43 per cent to 55 per cent; for all manufacturing, it rose from 38 per cent to 51 per cent. Within the food industry there have been some striking changes in the level of concentration ratios: for example bread and flour confectionery has risen from 24 per cent to 63 per cent; biscuits from 50 per cent to 83 per cent and confectionery from 41 per cent to 63 per cent. By any standards these are significant changes which are

1. Any views expressed in this paper are the responsibility of the author and do not necessarily reflect those of the Ministry of Agriculture, Fisheries and Food.

also apparent at the product level: the average five-firm product concentration ratio, that is the share of sales held by the five largest firms, has risen from 55 per cent in 1958 to 71 per cent in 1977 for food, whilst for all manufacturing it has increased from 55 per cent to 65 per cent. Several products which are common to most households have ratios of over 90 per cent, for example cereal breakfast foods, coffee, ice-cream, margarine, potato crisps and sugar. Whilst some care is required in the interpretation of concentration statistics, the overall evidence now seems to be suggesting that the rise in concentration, in both food manufacturing and the rest of manufacturing industry, may be levelling off; however, it is too early yet to be definite about this.

Changes in the level of concentration reflect changes that have taken place in company structure and activity. The past twenty years has been a period not only of internal growth for firms but one when there has been a considerable amount of merger and takeover activity. The number of food companies, defined in terms of turnover, in the top 50 United Kingdom companies in 1965 was three and in the top 200, fifteen; in 1980 these figures were seven and seventeen respectively. Some of these companies are conglomerates and care is needed in interpreting the statistics; however, one result of these changes is that today, the largest 100 United Kingdom enterprises in the private sector control about half of the sales of all United Kingdom food firms. Over this period, food companies have become increasingly diversified; the main areas of diversification have been drinks, in particular brewing, and leisure interests. Of the fifteen largest United Kingdom food firms in 1979, four had substantial drink interests and each of these diversified companies had been formed during the last twenty years. United Kingdom food firms have also been diversifying geographically by exporting and acquiring assets overseas. The result of this diversification is that of today's ten largest United Kingdom food manufacturing interests, it is estimated that only about a half of their sales are in food and two-thirds in food and drink: non-food interests have become a significant factor for "food" manufacturing companies.

ECONOMIC PERFORMANCE OF THE FOOD INDUSTRY

Over the past twenty years, the output of the food manufacturing industry has grown more slowly than for all manufacturing: 1980 has been an exception, when in the recession, food output has grown more rapidly. These trends are consistent with the relatively low income of elasticity of demand for food and the slow growth in the home population. With the oil and commodity prices boom in the mid-1970s and the United Kingdom decision to enter the EEC in 1973, food manufacturers, in common with all other industries, have faced a rapid change in their economic circumstances. Over the period 1960 to 1980, the real price of purchased inputs (materials, packaging and fuel) has risen at a slower rate for food than for the rest of manufacturing industry; a trend rate of +½ per cent per annum for food compared with +2 per cent per annum for the rest of industry. There are many reasons for this, including the oil-price explosion but it is interesting to note that the cost of agricultural raw materials, which comprise about one-third of all raw material purchases by manufacturing industry, has risen more slowly than the cost of the rest of manufacturing industry's raw material inputs.

Estimates made of productivity show that over this period total factor productivity has grown more slowly in the food industry than in all manufacturing; a trend rate of +0.8 per cent per annum for food compared with +1.3 per cent per annum for all manufacturing. Perhaps associated with this poorer productivity performance, the trend in the real price of output has been slightly upward for food and slightly downward for the rest of manufacturing industry. The profitability of food manufacturers has followed the long-run decline in profitability of all industries in the United Kingdom but the rate of return in food has generally been above the average for all manufacturing.

CONCLUSIONS

We have seen that the food industry is highly concentrated, more so than the all manufacturing average and that the level of concentration has risen significantly over the past twenty years. It is an industry that has experienced a considerable amount of merger and takeover activity, with the creation of a number of large, diversified companies. At the same time, there have been less favourable trends in productivity and output prices. The trend towards greater industrial concentration, accompanied by merger activity, is not unique to the food industry and care is needed in developing any causal links between these trends. However, whilst it is difficult to quantify the gains and losses resulting from the concentration of economic activity, economists are expected to enquire whether, or to what extent, the trend to greater industrial concentration, has been beneficial to the efficiency of the British economy: the importance of this question is not in doubt and it will continue to be the subject of debate amongst economists and others.

STRUCTURAL ADJUSTMENT OF THE FOOD INDUSTRIES OF THE UNITED STATES

by

John M. Connor
Economic Research Service
United States Department of Agriculture

INTRODUCTION

The purposes of this paper are to outline the major long-term changes in the structure of the United States food manufacturing industries, to identify the causes of change, to assess the implications of structural change for industry performance, and to discuss the efficacy of alternative public policies that might alleviate performance problems.

IMPORTANCE OF THE FOOD INDUSTRIES

Manufacturing contributed 25 per cent of gross United States product in 1978, and food manufacturing in turn originated 9.5 per cent of the national product generated by the manufacturing sector. However, in 1958 food manufacturing accounted for 12.2 per cent of the gross value added by manufacturing. On the basis of value added in 1978, only two of the other 19 manufacturing industries were larger.

In an international context the United States food processing industries rank quite high. Evaluated at official rates of exchange, the United Nations (1981) estimated that in 1975, the United States had the largest food processing sector of any market economy in the world (only that of the USSR might be larger), accounting for about 18 per cent of world production. United States food processing sales equalled about 80 per cent of all the Western European countries put together.

NUMBERS AND SIZE DISTRIBUTION OF FOOD FIRMS

Company numbers

The total number of food manufacturing firms in 1977 was slightly less than half the number in 1947. The rate of decline has averaged over 1 per cent per year in every period, peaking during 1963-67. The 20,616 companies remaining in 1977 includes every firm that has at least one production facility in food manufacturing. If one counts only firms that are principally engaged in food manufacturing, the 1977 total drops to 19,451 firms. The decline in the number of food firms stands in contrast to the rest of manufacturing where the number of companies has risen during every intercensal period except 1963-67.

The consolidation of ownership of the United States food industries can be traced in part to the breaking down of regional markets into national ones - a process that began in the late 19th century. Other factors that must be considered are increasing economies of scale in production and marketing and the very active merger period of the 1960s. Increasing economies of scale in production appear to be important in the dairy industries, some canning methods, flour milling, oil processing, and brewing. Mergers were at high levels in several food industries: dairy products, canned specialities, pasta products, and alcoholic beverages.

Concentration

Because smaller companies have been more affected, the decline in food company numbers has contributed to rising concentration.

Several different indexes have been developed to measure market concentration, but the most popular and accessible are the four-firm concentration ratios (CR4) published as part of the Census of Manufacturers. The CR4 is the sum of the shares of industry shipments of the four leading firms.

Weighted average national CR4 for the food manufacturing product classes in 1977 was 50.0 per cent. That is, on average the top four companies control exactly half of the markets for processed foods and beverages. As a "rule of thumb" economists often identify CR4 = 40 per cent as the critical level above which firms recognise their mutual dependence and begin to "co-ordinate" or "co-operate" in their business decision-making.

Market concentration of the food industries has increased over time according to every available data series. Average industry CR4 for food rose from 47 per cent in 1958 to 52 per cent in 1972.

Market concentration varies considerably among food manufacturing industries (Table 1). The least concentrated industry is sausages and prepared meats (CR4 = 22 per cent), while the most concentrated is chewing gum (CR4 = 93 per cent).

DIVERSIFICATION, AND PRODUCT DIFFERENTIATION

Product diversification

One of the outstanding features of competitive conduct in the United States food industries in the last 30 years is the vast sales diversification that has taken place among large companies. Food manufacturers have diversified both within food processing and outside the sector; moreover, nonfood firms have increasingly invested in the food industries. Out of the 20 major United States manufacturing groups, food ranks about 5th in the extent of employment diversification outside its principal enterprise industry; in 1954 food was one of the least diversified manufacturing industries.

Based on a study by Connor and MacDonald, something is known about the direction of diversification of major food manufacturers. Their principal area of manufacturing diversification in 1975 was chemicals, especially soaps and toiletries; fabricated metals and machinery are the second most popular area of investment. Outside of manufacturing, food companies have expanded mainly into wholesaling and retailing, especially eating places. In 1975, almost 3 per cent of the sales of the 200 largest food manufacturers were derived from United States foodservice operations, mostly fast-food chains.

Foreign direct investment (FDI) can be seen as an extension of national geographic expansion. FDI by United States firms abroad and FDI into the United States by foreign firms has been increasing at a rapid rate since the early 1960s. In the 1970s FDI into the United States food manufacturing industries rose by about 17 per cent per year; food ranks about third in FDI among the 20 manufacturing groups. Most FDI in the United States in 1977 came from Canada (33 per cent), Netherlands (32 per cent), the United Kingdom (16 per cent), Switzerland (14 per cent) and other European countries. Foreign-owned food affiliates tend to market highly differentiated products like tea, cookies, chocolate, alcoholic beverages, and the like.

Direct investment by United States companies in the food manufacturing industries of other countries is about three times as large as FDI into the United States. The rate of increase in United States FDI (about 12 per cent per year over 1966-79) is greater than domestic investment by less than inward FDI. Two-thirds of United States FDI lies in Canada and Western Europe.

Food product proliferation

The number of "new" food products, brands, and items introduced each year is very high according to most sources. During the 1970s at least 5,000 grocery items (food and nonfood) were introduced annually into warehouse distribution somewhere in the United States.

Advertising and promotion

Taken all together, total United States food and beverage advertising and sales promotion in 1979 amounted to at least $8 billion and possibly as high as $14 billion. In these totals, media advertising represents about 30 to 40 per cent of selling expenses.

FOOD INDUSTRY PERFORMANCE

Economic performance is a multidimentional phenomenon (Marion and Handy 1973). The various yardsticks of performance may all point in the same direction for a given industry, but trade-offs may need to be made in judging overall long-run performance. Moreover, there are numerous non-economic aspects of performance traditionally left unresearched by economists, partly because they seem non-quantifiable.

Profit performance

The profit rates of food manufacturers have increased steadily over the period 1951-1980. Profit rates (after deducting taxes) in the late 1970s averaged twice what they were in the early 1950s. Since 1970, the profits of food manufacturers exceeded the rest of manufacturing in most years.

Profit-market structure studies are the principal bases for asserting that some firms in some food industries possess market power. They are somewhat indirect tests of the core meaning of market power, the discretion over prices and insulation from changes in rivals' or inputs' prices.

Price performance

Parker and Connor (1979) regressed the price difference between national brands and private-label foods against food industry structure variables. The authors hypothesized that private-label food products are produced and marketed in order to sell at the lowest possible retail price - that is they are decent proxies for the cost of production (plus normal profits). On average, wholesale prices were 10 per cent higher than a workably competitive market structure would lead one to expect. The range, however, is enormous, with five of the 22 product classes exceeding the 20 per cent level.

Technological progressiveness

A third index of performance measures changes in the productivity of the food industries over time.

There are no empirical studies explaining variability in productivity rates among food industries, but Mueller, Culbertson, and Peckham (1979) did model the effect of food industry and firm organisation on R & D inputs and patent output.

Their results are not easy to summarise. As a broad generalisation, in large food industries (sales of $5 billion) maximum performance is reached with low concentration (CR4<50 per cent) and leading firms with less than $0.6 billion in assets each; in smaller industries ($0.5 to $1.0 billion) optimal progressiveness is reached with moderate concentration (60 per cent > CR4 > 40 per cent) and smaller leading firms ($50 to $150 million in assets). Technological progressiveness was also positively related to firm sales diversification.

Overall economic performance

In this section I take the doubtless controversial step of identifying the overall, long run, economic performance of specific United States food manufacturing industries. This categorisation is frankly based on a subjective weighting of several dimensions of structure and performance, especially profit rates, relative prices, the size of the competitive fringe, sales promotion costs, technical barriers to entry, and technological progress.

A rough categorisation of food industries by their overall quality of economic performance is hazarded in Table 1. Out of the 58 industries shown, five seem to me to be effective monopolies. Concentration and barriers to entry are high, price and profit performance are low, and there appear to be no redeeming dynamic factors. Another 28 industries depart significantly from the structural and performance standards of pure competition; 24 of these industries produce differentiated products, so some minor portion of industry output could be quite competitive. Eleven industries are in the main workably competitive - meeting most of the standards of good economic performance or reasonably competitive structure. Nine industries I have identified as near models of perfect competition insofar as the data at hand are accurate. For five industries, the indicators are changing so rapidly that judgment must be suspended.

CONCLUSION

In sum, in my opinion, slightly over half of the food industries exhibit significant performance problems warranting the attention of public policies. My review of the evidence convinces me that shortfalls in performance are largely due to structural features of these industries. Most of the industries have had oligopolistic structure-performance configurations for decades. This is not to say that antitrust and other "negative adjustment" policies have been completely ineffective, but rather than halting the drift toward monopoly, they have merely slowed it. Alternative United States policies promoting competition (positive adjustment) have been rather ineffective. I include in this category small business or co-operative subsidies, import competition, public food price and quality information for consumers, research on smaller-scale production techniques, and others.

Table 1

WEIGHTED AVERAGE FOUR-FIRM SALES CONCENTRATION IN THE UNITED STATES FOOD AND TOBACCO MANUFACTURING INDUSTRIES, 1977

SIC No.	Industry	Value of shipments(1)	Value added (2)	Four-firm concentration ratio(3)
		Million dollars		Per cent
2011	Meatpacking	21,414	4,010	28.8
2013	Sausages and prepared meats	9,748	2,039	22.3
2016	Poultry dressing	5,834	1,237	29.0
2017	Egg processing	313	192	30.0
2021	Butter	1,110	75	30.0
2022	Cheese, natural and processed	5,245	949	45.0
2023	Condensed and evaporated milk	2,966	805	43.7
2024	Ice cream and frozen desserts	2,230	664	68.0
2026	Fluid milk	10,867	3,176	66.0
2032	Canned soup, baby food, etc.	2,430	1,143	68.5
2033	Canned fruits and vegetables	6,312	2,542	42.2
2034	Dried fruits and vegetables	1,123	473	46.8
2035	Pickles, sauces, and dressings	2,107	987	53.4
2037	Frozen fruits and vegetables	2,951	1,323	34.8
2038	Frozen specialities	2,786	1,218	50.3
2041	Flour and other grain mill products	3,176	825	42.2
2043	Breakfast cereals	1,833	1,447	81.0
2044	Milled rice	1,242	341	47.0
2045	Flour mixes and refrigerated doughs	1,492	490	48.0
2046	Wet corn milling	1,946	667	61.0
2047	Pet food	2,985	1,393	55.8
2048	Prepared feeds	7,328	1,545	63.0
2051	Bread, cake	7,340	5,377	57.0
2052	Cookies, crackers	2,747	1,696	61.4
2061	Raw cane sugar	798	276	42.0
2062	Refined cane sugar	2,168	526	63.0
2063	Refined beet sugar	1,160	345	67.0
2065	Confections	3,955	2,028	47.6
2066	Chocolate and cocoa	1,794	641	71.8
2067	Chewing gum	649	336	93.0
2074	Cottonseed oil, partly refined	750	197	45.7
2075	Soybean oil, partly refined	6,087	374	50.4
2076	Vegetable oil, partly refined	370	58	53.2
2077	Animal and marine fats and oils	1,994	584	25.5
2079	Shortening and cooking oils	4,237	692	50.3
2082	Brewing	6,590	2,602	66.4
2083	Malt	489	101	60.0
2084	Wines, brandy	1,358	510	52.0
2085	Distilled liquors	1,909	1,150	54.0
2086	Bottled and canned soft drinks	8,504	4,085	86.0
2087	Flavouring extracts and syrups	2,422	1,453	74.8
2091	Canned and cured seafood	1,026	441	37.0
2092	Fresh or frozen packaged fish	2,093	706	26.5
2095	Roasted coffee	5,062	988	64.7
2097	Manufactured ice	141	106	22.0
2098	Macaroni, spaghetti, noodles	752	327	32.0
2099	Food preparations NEC	5,577	3,028	61.7
20	Total food	167,315	56,062	50.0
2011	Cigarettes	6,098	3,803	88.0
2121	Cigars	256	126	54.0
2131	Chewing and smoking tobacco, snuff	401	189	65.0
2141	Tobacco stemming and redrying	1,702	217	71.5
21	Total tobacco	8,458	4,334	82.6

1. Value of product shipments, less Census "NSK" (not specified by kind) product classes, as shown in Tables 9 and 10 of source.
2. Value added on an industry basis, from the General Summary.
3. Weighted by value of product class shipments, excluding "NSK" classes. Some estimated values, including for four local-market industries.

Sources: Census (1977b) tables 9 and 10 and Census (1977).

THE ADJUSTMENT OF THE YUGOSLAV AGRO-KOMBINATS TO THE CHALLENGE OF THE 1980s

by

Mr. Vladimir Cvetkovic
Institute for Foreign Trade Research
Belgrade, Yugoslavia

Of the total of 7.5 million ha. of arable land, the socialised sector disposes of about 15 per cent. The biggest Agro-Kombinats (the "big five", all situated in Vojvodina and Slovenia)(1) possess about one-half of the socialised area. Their influence on the country's agriculture, which achieved about 10 million tonnes of maize, 6 million tonnes of wheat, about 850,000 tonnes of sugar, 270,000 tonnes of edible oil, 1.3 million tonnes of meat and 4 million tonnes of milk - is of the greatest importance. The modern technology and organisation of the work, the consequence of which are the high yields and high productivity in fattening livestock, are transferred to the private sector often through the various forms of co-operation.

Not only the big Kombinats, which possess over 40-50,000 ha. each (some of them have 100,000 ha.), but the smaller ones too are integrated enterprises, having production as well as processing capacity (slaughterhouses, dairies, mills, industry for oil extraction, sugar factories, compound feed factories). Both branches of production - raw materials and processed commodities - enables them to be large exporters. In total Yugoslav exports of agricultural and food commodities of 1.2 billion dollars, the Agro-Kombinats have about a 50 per cent share.

Having in mind the promising prospects for food demand in the world market in the eighties as well the still unexploited possibilities of the Yugoslav Agro-Kombinats (and Yugoslav agriculture in general), the exports of food could achieve a value of 2 billion dollars in 1985. In addition, through tourism, food "exports" could bring 600-700 million dollars, since

1. Except PK "BEOGRAD" which is near BEOGRAD.

food consumption accounts for about one-third of the total spent by foreign tourists. The export of technology and know-how could bring additional foreign currency.

In order to be capable of meeting the challenge of the eighties, the Agro-Kombinats of Yugoslavia have to do the following:

- to enlarge their area by up to 250,000 ha. and to increase production of cereals, oilseeds, sugar beets and animal feed;
- to revive stockbreeding, especially cattle breeding, in order to exploit their own potentialities in animal feed production;
- to improve integrated production processes and to create production lines (animal feed - young livestock production - animal fattening - animal slaughtering - meat processing - distribution and export) and to expand the liberal and clear market relations among the partners under one roof;
- to make strong link with individual farmers which held about 85 per cent of the land and 95 per cent of livestock, especially those willing to apply new technology, use high yielding plants and to breed high productivity animals.

Through their new "image", the Yugoslav Agro-Kombinats could easily play a role as the engine of growth for exports. They could contribute possibly 50 per cent of the projected increase in 2 billion dollars by 1985. Their participation could also expand invisible exports through foreign tourism (about 300 million dollars), so that Agro-Kombinat exports could achieve a value of about 1.3 billion dollars. Further sums could result from the export of technology and know-how to the developing countries.

B. PRESENTATION AND DISCUSSION OF A CASE STUDY FOR A MULTINATIONAL FOOD FIRM

"The Experience of Cadbury Schweppes Ltd."

by

Sir Adrian Cadbury
Chairman of the Food and Drinks Industries Council
United Kingdom

The British food industry has radically altered its structure over the last thirty years. The most obvious change is the increase in concentration in manufacturing and in distribution; the movement in the two sectors clearly being related.

In the first place all the large companies have broken out of their original product boundaries. They are no longer the bread, beer, milk, meat or confectionery companies they were only a relatively short time ago - they are food and drink companies. Secondly this process of expansion across market boundaries has enabled them to develop their businesses overseas at a faster rate and so has significantly strengthened Britain's standing in the international league table - some 20 out of the top 100 food companies in the world are British.

The Cadbury business started in 1824 when my great-grandfather opened a grocer's shop in the centre of Birmingham with the manufacture of cocoa soon becoming his main business. In 1879 my grandfather moved the business from the centre of Birmingham some four miles out to Bournville, where our main confectionery factory stands today.

Between the two World Wars the Commonwealth countries raised tariffs against imports and so the Cadbury company set up factories overseas. Cadbury became an international business, in the sense of having a number of subsidiary companies outside the United Kingdom, not as a result of a considered strategy but as a reluctant response to political action.

In 1962 Cadbury became a publicly quoted company, because there is a limit to the time which a company can remain in family hands and by then we had members of the fifth generation of the family working in the business. As a public company the short-term dependence of the business on a volatile commodity like cocoa required us to widen our product range. We went into sugar confectionery, chocolate biscuits, cakes, milk products, potato products and even to a modest extent into meat.

The merger with Schweppes came about in 1969. Both Cadbury and Schweppes had reduced their dependence on their main businesses of confectionery and soft drinks by developing food divisions. Neither food business however was large enough on its own to be an effective force in the British grocery market. At the same time both companies faced international competitors with greater resources than they had. Combining the two businesses was a direct way of meeting their separate objectives:-

- the new company was broadly based: instead of each of the partners having a main and a subsidiary business Cadbury Schweppes had three major divisions - confectionery, drinks and food;
- the two companies were reasonably complementary in terms of their overseas markets: Schweppes was strong in the United States and Europe, Cadbury in the Commonwealth; we could therefore build a combined business in any market where only one of the partners had been established before;
- combined the two companies had the financial resources to invest in marketing, in manufacturing, and in research and development on a scale to compete with their international competitors;
- both companies marketed branded goods and their main assets lay in the Cadbury and Schweppes brands they had built up; they therefore had the same approach to business and to the development of their markets.

It is now possible to see major benefits from the merger in terms of the better use of manpower and of production facilities (Chart 1).

We have had three main objectives in Cadbury Schweppes since 1975:

- to invest consistently in the marketing and manufacture of our major international brands;

Chart 1 **CADBURY SCHWEPPES**

UNITED KINGDOM EMPLOYEES

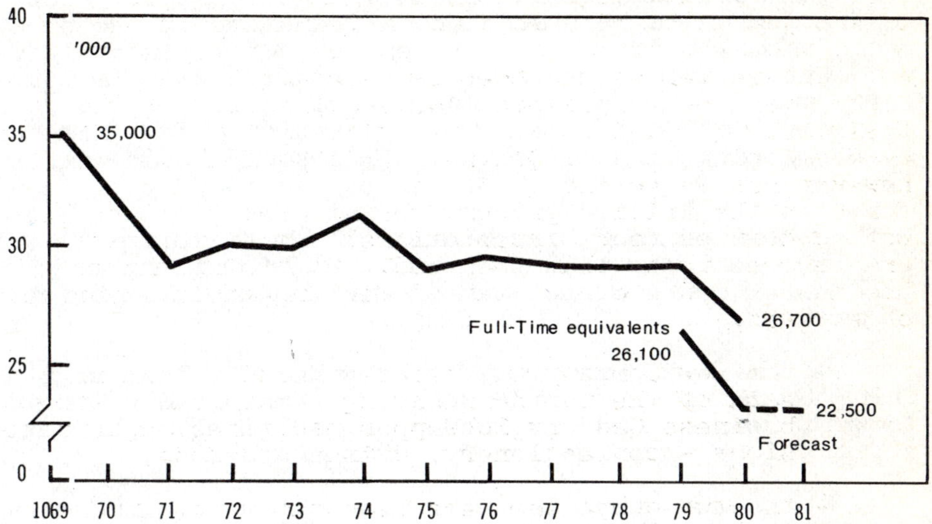

UNITED KINGDOM FACTORIES

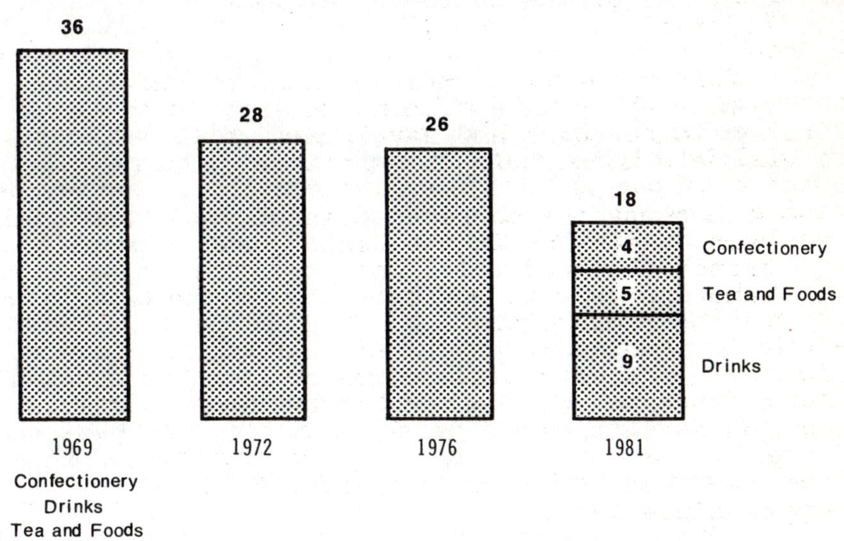

- to change the geographical balance of the business by putting additional investment into North America and Continental Europe;

- to improve the efficiency with which we use the assets tied up in the business.

The first and third objectives go together. Concentration on major brands and a reduction in the product range makes it feasible to invest in a few, automated production layouts, which in turn require less factory space and a smaller workforce. As a result of this policy of concentration the return on operating assets has risen steadily from 13.7 per cent in 1977 to 18.6 per cent in 1980.

On the geographical balance of the business (Chart 2), the degree of change can be measured by comparison with 1977 when 7 per cent of sales were in North America and 61 per cent in the United Kingdom.

On the basis of the experience of the food and drink industry in Britain, what are some of the issues to which we, as food companies, should be directing our attention in planning for the future?

First what kind of economic environment will we be operating in? I assume that the next decade will be a period of slow growth, of financial instability and of severe competition. Will as a result the world move in the direction of protection and nationalism or towards freer trade?

Secondly for those food companies based in Europe how will the CAP be modified? Will it continue to be irreconcilably an instrument of social as well as agricultural policy? If so, we can expect that our input costs will be higher and our exports less competitive than those of our international competitors; but we need to take a view on how wide the gap will be between EEC and world agricultural prices in the long run.

A third question is what will the impact of innovation and of technological progress be on our industry? Bio-technology has the potential to alter the face of the industry even more fundamentally than the application of micro-electronics. The food industry is likely to be employing fewer people directly during the next decade; what are the social and economic implications of this decline in employment?

A further issue for food manufacturers is how the earnings derived from the sale of food to the consumer will be divided between them, the producers and the distributors? Producers have political power; distributors have market power; the manufacturer is uneasily placed between these two powerful groups.

A final issue we need to consider is the way our businesses should be organised and managed to cope with changing markets and with changing attitudes towards industry. How should international companies ensure that their operations outside Europe retain the goodwill and support of their host communities? What about the problems of size; at what point does a company become too large to be effective in business or in human terms?

Chart 2 **CADBURY SCHWEPPES**

£ 1,271 m WORLD-WIDE SALES BY PRODUCT GROUP 1981

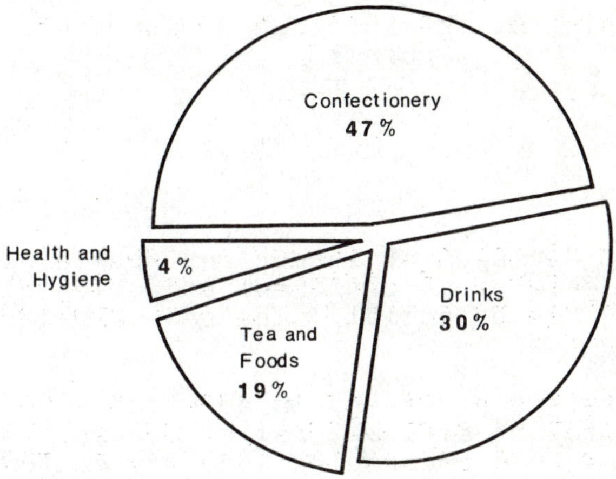

SALES £ 1,271 m 1981

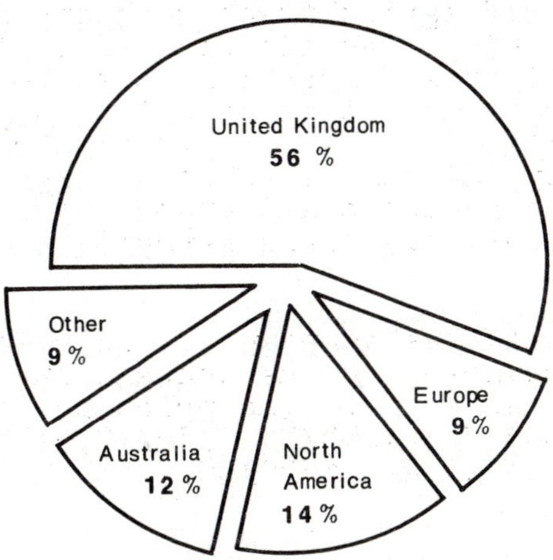

C. ADDITIONAL PAPER

EUROPEAN COMMUNITY ACTION FOR STRUCTURAL IMPROVEMENT IN THE MARKETING OF AGRICULTURAL PRODUCTS

by

Mr. B. Huber
Commission of the European Communities
Brussels

Increasing division of labour and specialisation are essential features of efficient economies with good income and earnings potential. The same applies to the agricultural sector.

It is therefore necessary in adopting a modern approach to policy on agricultural structure, to pay due attention to the food processing industry as the farmers' first and largest customer. An efficient food industry - together with its marketing facilities - ensures:

- optimum producer prices with narrow processing margins. This aspect is receiving increasing attention against the background of pressure for a prudent price policy in the Community;
- the sale of agricultural products in and outside the Community. An efficient food industry is essential if intervention is to be reduced in favour of a long-term export strategy as a means of dealing with the structural surpluses in the Community, all the more so as high-value-added processed products and other luxury goods account for a relatively large percentage of Community exports.

The Community has adopted guidance measures for structural improvement in the concentration of supply, processing and marketing. The principal legal bases are Regulations (EEC) No. 1035/72, 355/77, 1360/78, 1361/78, 1945/81 and parts of No. 1820/80.

Council Regulations (EEC) Nos. 1035/72, 1360/78 and 1943/81 were adopted to make good the structural deficiencies detected in the supply and marketing of certain agricultural products.

The concentration of supply and certain ties between growers on the one hand and the processing industry and marketing channels on the other ensure sales, regulate the flow of goods and stabilize the market. There is thus a logical connection between Regulations (EEC) No. 1360/78 and No. 355/77.

The Community's aim in Regulation (EEC) No. 355/77 (as amended by Regulation 1361/78) is to facilitate the adaptation of agriculture to the economic consequences of the Common Agricultural Policy or its requirements by modernising and rationalising treatment and processing and/or marketing establishments. The prime consideration is thus farming and farm incomes.

In order to improve the efficiency of the aid measure, furnish evidence of the need for Community aid in areas with the greatest structural deficiencies and indicate possible medium-term solutions, the Member States are required under Regulation (EEC) No. 355/77 to draw up appropriate specific programmes. Target capacities must be in line with the raw materials produced in the programme area. Processing in the area of production is generally cheaper and thus more profitable for the growers.

In order to safeguard the close connection between production and processing/marketing, only programmes and projects relating to products listed in Annex II to the Treaty are eligible for aid.

So far, (situation at 31st December, 1981) 114 programmes with a total investment of 7,072 million ECU have been approved by Commission Decisions, 52 per cent of the planned investment being in the three sectors - milk, fruit and vegetables and meat. Further details of the breakdown by Member States, the general guidelines followed in programmes in individual sectors and the investment involved are given in the table attached to this paper.

The programmes submitted by the Member States generally indicate a large investment requirement on the part of the food industry. Only some of the projects can be granted aid from the EAGGF, which has about 150 million ECU a year available for this purpose. The EAGGF contribution to the projects ranges from 25 per cent to 50 per cent in areas where the situation is particularly difficult.

The product categories covered by the proposed structural improvement and production orientation are as follows: eleven programmes approved in the milk and milk products sector account for a total investment of 1,346 million ECU, a large part of which, however, is excluded from subsequent project aid as being incompatible with the objectives of the Common Agricultural Policy. The main aim of the milk programme is modernisation and rationalisation of the existing capacity.

In view of the problems of disposing of milk and milk products, the Commission, when assessing the individual aims of programmes, has allowed no overall increase in milk processing capacity, giving preference to more marketable goods (especially new products and certain varieties of cheese).

There is, however, provision for some exceptions in favour of particularly disadvantaged areas, as there is in all other sectors with a restrictive investment aid policy.

As for the fruit and vegetables sector, the Commission has so far approved 24 programmes, representing a total investment of 1,301 million ECU. Priority has been given to storage and marketing facilities for fresh produce. Apart from new products, some specialities, juices and frozen products, the Commission has permitted no increase in capacity, paying particular attention to tomatoes, peaches and pears.

As regards slaughterhouses and meat processing plants, the Commission has so far approved thirteen programmes, representing a total investment of 839 million ECU. With the exception of some regions, the Community has a surplus capacity for slaughtering.

The programmes are therefore confined to structural improvements in the slaughterhouse sector, with no increase in overall capacity, and are aimed at achieving optimum production units with specialised slaughter lines. Slaughterhouse programmes often also cover meat processing, including the requisite cold stores and packaging facilities.

With eight approved programmes and a total investment of over 849 million ECU, the wine sector also occupies a prominent position in the implementation of Regulation (EEC) No. 355/77. The programmes concentrate on structural improvement by means of eliminating processing establishments which are too small, without increasing processing capacity overall. Additional storage capacity is to be created under the programmes to offset fluctuations in production and quality. Aid is confined to the production of high-quality wines.

ASSESSMENT OF THE EFFICIENCY OF THE "COMMON MEASURES" TO IMPROVE MARKETING STRUCTURE

Regulation (EEC) No. 355/77 meets a need in all Member States, which is shown, among other things, by the fact that the number of programmes and projects submitted far exceeds the budget available. Rapidly changing marketing and consumer requirements call for a special intensity of investment to maintain outlets and competitiveness, in order to provide the consumer with high-quality foodstuffs and ensure the narrowest possible margins.

Table 1

AMOUNT OF INVESTMENT IN PROGRAMMES ADOPTED
(Breakdown according to Member State and Product)

(Mill. ECU)

Product / Member State	B	DK	D	EL	F	IRL	I	L	NL	UK	Total
Cereals	20	-	79	137	97	50	-	-	-	52	435
Potatoes	18	44	87	-	-	49	-	-	-	52	250
Oilseeds and oleaginous plants	-	-	-	134	-	-	65	-	-	-	199
Tobacco	-	-	2	-	-	-	80	-	-	-	82
Seed	13	25	46	-	93	-	-	-	4	10	191
Fruit and vegetables	46	52	284	213	192	-	350	-	90	74	1,301
Wine	-	-	264	37	337	-	200	11	-	-	849
Cultivation of ornamental plants, nurseries	6	-	28	-	40	-	-	-	113	-	187
Meat	76	172	61	-	191	192	-	-	29	118	839
Milk	96	265	327	-	209	185	-	-	46	218	1,346
Eggs and poultry meat	20	7	9	-	137	4	-	-	24	-	201
Livestock production, mixed programmes	-	-	8	-	-	-	290	-	-	-	298
Fisheries	-	72	48	-	-	43	115	-	11	64	353
Others, including multisectoral programmes	10	50	-	-	226	-	-	-	-	255	541
Total	305	687	1,243	521	1,522	523	1,100	11	317	843	7,072

II. CHANGES IN THE RELATIONS BETWEEN FOOD PROCESSING AND AGRICULTURAL PRODUCTION, FOOD DISTRIBUTION AND CONSUMPTION

A. Relation between Food Processing Industries Production and Distribution for Selected Commodities

A DANISH CASE STUDY IN THE DAIRY AND BACON SECTORS

by

Mr. B. Folmer Pedersen
Ministry of Agriculture
Denmark

The summary indicates the importance of producer co-operatives in the Danish dairy and bacon factory sector, and focusses on recent structural changes both horizontally and vertically.

In the 1950s Danish dairy processing consisted of many similar small enterprises all of which produced almost the same range of products. Technical developments and efforts to rationalise both the collecting of raw milk and the processing and distribution of consumer-ready products have resulted in the establishment of larger production plants and distribution units. Concentration trends have been strongest in the processing of liquid milk where the processing and sales have become increasingly integrated. Even with the growth of larger associations, there remain a great number of minor and small enterprises, especially within the production of butter and cheese.

In the financial year 1979/80 (milk year) 42 per cent of the total milk quantity was collected by 7 companies each collecting more than 100 million kg; 13 per cent of the milk was collected by 111 companies each collecting less than 10 million kg. The private part of the Danish dairy sector produces a relatively large part of the processed dairy products considering its share of the total collected milk quantity. This may be seen from the table in the annex.

The three largest dairy associations are Mejeriselskabet Danmark A.m.b.a. (MD), Øernes Konsummaelkselskab A.m.b.a. (ØKS), and Kløvermaelk A.m.b.a. (A.m.b.a = co-operative company). The latter is a co-operative venture between a number of independent dairies and dairy companies in Jylland, which market their liquid milk products under the common brand "Kløvermaelk".

As transport of liquid milk is rather expensive the distribution is divided geographically. West of Store Baelt, MD and Kløvermaelk dominate with 40 and 50 per cent respectively of the production while on Sjaelland MD and ØKS are taking over production to an increasing degree. Nearly all the liquid milk is sold on the domestic market. After the cancellation of the milk agreements there is now free entry to the wholesale and retail trade in milk. This has not resulted in an involvement in the retail trade by the dairies, rather the big food chains have become interested in the processing link. As regards butter, the distribution to the retail outlets is done largely by the dairies themselves. Andelssmør A.m.b.a., of which MD holds 20 per cent, has a share of 95 per cent of exports of butter.

Similar to the dairy sector, concentration has increased on the supply side in the pig meat sector as total production has increased. Today roughly 8 per cent of the suppliers produce about 48 per cent of the total number of pigs. The number of slaughterhouse companies has been reduced from 77 in 1962 to 19 in 1981 and at the same time the number of slaughtering units has fallen from 77 to 35. Technical developments have made many slaughtering units unprofitable and that is the reason for their closure. Mergers between companies must be seen in the light of the efforts to make the most of the remaining capacity. Developments since 1962 are summarised in the table in the annex.

In terms of exports, all export authorised slaughterhouses are affiliated to the sales association ESS-Food. The members have given ESS-Food a monopoly in the export of whole pigs and bacon for the United Kingdom, Ireland and for countries with centralised buying. ESS-Food handles 83 per cent of Danish pork exports. Individual slaughterhouses handle the remaining exports themselves, mainly of canned meat and parts of pork. The sale of fresh pork on the domestic market takes place either directly to the retail trade or through buying associations. Wholesale grocers play an unimportant role. Branded goods are widespread [e.g. Tulip (co-op), Plumrose, Normeat (private)].

As regards distribution, today the typical retailer/supermarket/minimarket obtains its daily supplies from 5 to 6 different suppliers. As a consequence of the rise in transport costs following the oil crisis, this expensive form of distribution will change through the establishment of a system of fresh goods terminals. These terminals will provide storage for fresh goods e.g. fresh meat, dairy products, fresh fruit and vegetables, bread, and fresh fish. A terminal system covering all the goods mentioned would mean that the retailer would receive a single daily "package" of all these goods. Initially, the terminal system will handle the distribution of dairy products and fresh meat only, but the aim is to expand it to all the above mentioned products.

The impact of this system on the Danish food distribution will depend on three factors viz: the range of products (i.e. the wider the range of products in the terminal the greater the attractiveness to retailers), the number of retailers willing to obtain supplies from the terminals and the number of producers wishing to provide supplies to the terminals.

It is maintained that the terminals' primary aim is to serve supermarkets. An agreement with FDB secures the terminal system a share of 25 per cent of sales of the goods in question, but the degree of support for the system at the retail level is uncertain. Wholesalers and buying associations have disassociated themselves from the idea. The grocers fear the loss of free choice in suppliers, especially for dairy products. They also fear that the only future supplier will be HD (the company Hjemmemarkedsselskabet Danmark established with the purpose of managing the fresh goods terminal system) which has also entered into close co-operation with the greatest competitor to the grocers viz. FDB.

The fresh goods terminals will undoubtedly strengthen the position of the producers involved. Producers who are outside the system will see their bargaining position weakened. Producers outside the circle of the slaughterhouses and dairies choosing to supply the terminals may be forced to give up country-wide distribution of their own brands.

Compared with FDB-Brugsen, voluntary chains will be minor customers and thus in a weak bargaining position vis-à-vis the terminals. To the minor retailers, grocers, bakers, and slaughterers, the terminals will probably mean increasing prices because of the costs in connection with distribution outside the terminal system. This may result in an acceleration of the development towards a retail trade structure mainly composed of large units and chains. This may result in a further weakening of the wholesale link as large units may tend to deal directly with producers or producer associations rather than with wholesalers.

Annex

DISTRIBUTION OF COLLECTED MILK QUANTITY AND PRODUCTION AMONG CO-OPERATIVE COMPANIES AND PRIVATE COMPANIES 1979/80
(Per Cent)

	Co-operative	Private
The collected milk quantity	87	13
Butter production	93	7
Cheese production	78	22
Liquid milk production	81	19
Preserved milk products	50	50+)

+) 1978/79

NUMBER OF DAIRY COMPANIES PRODUCING VARIOUS TYPES OF DAIRY PRODUCTS

	Co-operative	Private
Butter	132	34
Cheese	94	47
Liquid milk	55	20
Preserved milk products	10	7

Source: Mejeristatistik no. 2, March 1981.

NUMBER OF SLAUGHTERHOUSES 1962-1981

Companies	1962	1970	1977	1978	1979	1980	1981
Co-op with more than one slaughter unit	0	1	10	9	10	11	9
Co-op with one slaughter unit only	62	49	12	11	10	7	8
Total No. of co-ops.	62	50	22	20	20	18	17
Privately owned slaughterhouses(1)	15	4	3	3	2	2	2
Total number of companies	77	54	25	23	22	20	19
Slaughtering units							
Number of co-ops.	62	56	35	33	34	34	33
Number of privately owned units(1)	15	4	4	4	3	2	2
Total number of units	77	60	39	37	37	36	35
Number of units in companies with more than one unit		7	23	24	26	27	25

1. From 1st January Herning slaughterhouses is a partly co-operative slaughterhouse.

Source: Statistik 1980, Eksportsvineslagteriernes brancheudvalg.

CHANGES IN THE RELATIONS BETWEEN AGRICULTURAL PRODUCERS, PROCESSORS AND DISTRIBUTORS: A CASE STUDY FOR THE INDUSTRIAL VEGETABLES, SLAUGHTER CATTLE AND MEAT IN THE FEDERAL REPUBLIC OF GERMANY

by

Dr. D. Goeman and J. Roggenkamp
Ministry of Food, Agriculture and Forestry
Germany

In the Federal Republic of Germany in the case of food products some major shifts in the consumption of food products are being reflected in the intake of protein-rich food, in particular meat and meat products, and in vitamin-rich food, in particular fruit and vegetables.

Apart from a strong demand for greater convenience, the bridging of seasons when lower supplies of fresh fruit and vegetables are available continues to play an important role. The high consumption of meat products and especially sausages is a peculiarity of the German market and is connected with the consumption habits for breakfast and evening meals (Table 1). As in the fruit and vegetable sectors, there has been an increase in the share by value of semi-processed and processed meat (meat products) compared to fresh meat.

The greatest changes in food marketing in the Federal Republic of Germany have undoubtedly resulted from changes in the food retailing structure, mainly the increase in business concentration. In retailing, many small enterprises have disappeared and large enterprises have substantially expanded their share of sales by introducing new business practices.

Despite this development, the butchers, who compete not only with meat processing enterprises in the meat processing function, but also in their selling function with the meat departments of the larger retail stores, have maintained their position surprisingly well. The number of firms has declined, but sales have expanded substantially and additional personnel employed.

Table 1

CONSUMER EXPENDITURE BY THE MEDIAN HOUSEHOLD
DM per month(1)

Commodity Group	1962/ 1963	1978	1978 over 1962/63 (%)
	(DM/Month)		
Total food, beverages and tobacco	294.20	563.30	+91
Total food	216.90	355.80	+64
of which: meat and meat products	67.70	120.60	+78
Share of meat products	41%	47%	-
of which: fruit and vegetables	27.80	45.40	+63
Share of canned, preserves, deep frozen goods	26%	34%	-
Consumption in restaurants etc.	28.40	113.10	+298

1. Results derived from a random sample.

Apart from suppliers of weekly markets, which provide an important source of fresh fruit and vegetables, fruit and vegetable shops are now rare. In the more speciality retail stores, the departments for fresh fruit and vegetables are particularly attractive to customers. In contrast, discounters and chain stores who concentrated on rapid turnover and goods without handling problems, are selling a high percentage of canned fruit and vegetables. Since these outlets attach special importance to obtaining their products on the most favourable terms, German producers of canned vegetables are exposed to the exercise of substantial bargaining power by canned product buyers.

The distinction between food retailing and wholesaling is becoming increasingly blurred because of the integration which has taken place in the last two decades. All large groupings of retailers have close connections with purchasing centers at the wholesale level.

In the food processing and manufacturing industries, the number of enterprises has been declining for many years, as has the number of employed persons. Simultaneously, however, sales have been increasing so that the sales per employed person have increased substantially. According to the Monopoly Commission in 1977, the turnover concentration in the German food processing and manufacturing industries as a whole is still relatively low. In the two sectors examined in greater detail, concentration is, however, far above average. The 10 largest enterprises for fruit and vegetable processing account for about 50 per cent of sales and for the meat processing industry for about 26 per cent of sales.

The developments outlined above have had an impact on those involved in product assembly and upon agricultural producers. The intervention guarantee provided through EC market organisation has on the whole played an important role in protecting the market position of farmers, its impact is, however, more indirect for livestock and meat and for fruit and vegetables, in particular, those for canning. The abolition of import quotas under the EC-market organisation for fruit and vegetables forced the German canning business to cope with greater competition. The prices offered were often not satisfactory to farmers; consequently they switched their production to products with a stricter price support (e.g. grains or sugar beet). As a result contract cultivation of the most important vegetables declined (Table 2).

Table 2

DEVELOPMENT OF CONTRACT CULTIVATION OF THE MOST IMPORTANT VEGETABLES(HA)

Vegetables	1975	1978	1978 over 1975
Early carrots	334	229	68.6%
Late carrots	1184	1118	94.4%
Small early carrots	736	689	93.6%
Small late carrots	734	748	101.9%
Small peas	4693	4415	91.4%
French beans	5234	4805	91.8%

Source: Statistisches Bundesamt.

This perhaps explains why the German fruit and vegetable processing industry has fully exploited the increase in the demand for its products. It has lost market shares to foreign countries and has tried to shift its production programme to higher-price quality lines (Table 3). The situation in the fruit and vegetable canning industries has reached such a state that the Federal Government has made great efforts to determine the causes of this inadequate competitiveness. The reasons are mainly to be found in the inadequate structure of the industry and its weak marketing effort. Recognising the problems which exist, industry has recently launched a model project in the canned vegetable sector with a view to inducing individual firms to co-operate in joint marketing efforts.

Table 3

SHARE OF VEGETABLES IMPORTS IN TOTAL CONSUMPTION
Percentages

	1969/1970	1970	1974/1975	1975	1979/1980	1980
Canned peas	70.6		85.8		96.6	
Canned beans	58.8		68.1		73.4	
Total canned vegetables	63.5		79.8		83.5	
Deep-frozen vegetables		19.6		34.1		n.a.
Canned gherkins		16.0		20.1		17.0
Pickled vegetables		22.4		20.6		16.0

Source: Bundesverband der obst- und gemüseverarbeitenden Industrie e.V.

n.a. Not available

The structure of West German slaughter cattle marketing has undergone a radical change in the post-war period. After refrigeration techniques were improved and slaughter cattle became more sensitive to transport costs, slaughterings became increasingly concentrated in regions away from consumption areas. The concentration in meat marketing and the expansion of distribution through general food retailers have favoured this development. Accordingly, traditional slaughter cattle marketing through public slaughterhouses has declined in importance (Table 4). Butchers and wholesale slaughterers have also declined in importance in livestock and meat marketing relative to private and co-operative slaughterhouses and meat products factories.

With the decline of slaughter cattle supplies in central and medium-sized markets serious problems in pricing arose. A number of disturbances occurred in the Federal Republic of Germany which contributed to disquiet among livestock producers and affected slaughter marketing and payment according to the quality of carcasses. Often producer organisations through their representatives sought to prevent manipulation at the point of sale. This caused the Federal Government to initiate an amendment to the Livestock and Meat Act, with the intention of restricting substantially the possibility of manipulation. In summary, the retail trade has met the demands of consumers as far as possible with regard to cheap supply and greater convenience which has favoured an increase in the services provided by the food processing industry. For the Government, the problem is to monitor the balance of market forces and, if necessary, to take measures to improve the functioning of these forces in the product areas of fruit and vegetables and in livestock and meat.

Table 4

ORIGIN OF MEAT PRODUCTION
(As percentage of total meat products)

	1955	1970	1980
Home slaughterings	20	10	6.2
Butchers	43	30	35.8 (Butchers and Medium-sized markets)
Medium-sized markets	30 (Medium-sized and Central markets)	25 (Medium-sized and Central markets)	
Central markets			4.0
Private and co-operative Slaughterhouses and Meat Processing Industry	7	35	54.0

Source: Probst, F.W., Vermarktungskosten und Spannen bei Ring- und Schweinefleisch - Trend zu Bestimmungsfaktoren, IFLMF 1976, S. 37 and Federal Ministry calculations.

THE RELATIONS BETWEEN AGRI-BUSINESS AND AGRICULTURAL PRODUCERS A CASE STUDY ON VEAL CALVES, BROILERS AND PIGS IN THE NETHERLANDS

by

Mr. J. J. de Vlieger
Agricultural Economics Research Institute
The Hague

In this paper we will study major structural developments and their consequences for the relations between agricultural producers and their market partners. Finally we will turn our attention to expected developments and the possible policies for the 1980s.

STRUCTURAL CHANGES DURING THE 1970s

While agricultural production increased, the number of farms fell, causing average production per farm to rise sharply. There has also been an increase in the number of specialised farms. The percentage of specialised slaughter pig holdings increased from 6 per cent to 15 per cent of all slaughter pig holdings.

In agri-business the processing firms also have had an increase in the scale of the production. The co-operatives have an important market share in total agri-business. Their market share in the production of compound feed was for instance 53 per cent in 1979 and in the production of poultry 32 per cent. Furthermore the processing firms have added more services to their products and are applying more product differentiation. As a result of mergers there exist organisational linkages between all kinds of processing firms.

MARKET BEHAVIOUR AND RELATIONS

Competition

In both the short and long term, farmers are loyal to their market partners. Most of them sell their products to one buyer during the year and have had such a relationship with their buyer for at least five years.

The required investments necessitate that processing firms utilise their capacity as fully as possible and so they strive to maintain and enlarge their market share. Thus they wish to retain client loyalty. This is done via - product differentiation (selling under brand names, giving their clients service) - price discounts and bonuses.

These discounts and bonuses are determined by differences in costs and competitive conditions. So most producers receive a bonus on the price for the bulk of their slaughter pigs. The most important type of bonus is the quantum bonus for the number of pigs delivered during the year.

Price discovery systems

In the pig, broiler and veal calf sector various types of price discovery systems exist. The producer of compound feed usually fixes the price on the basis of costs, plus a margin (administered pricing). The price for broilers and slaughter pigs is mostly based on private marketwide supply and demand estimation by slaughterers. For veal calves and breeding pigs, dispersed direct trading is used, for newly born calves central trading on markets. In the case of fattening pigs and day-old chicks the price is often based on formulas relating to selling prices and costs in the different production stages. The purpose is to distribute the total returns as fairly as possible over the production stages. In formula and administered pricing there is a tendency for prices to be relatively stable. In terms of the market position of the farmer, market information collected and published by independent institutions and the activities of co-operatives are both important.

Co-ordination

Markets change continuously, so production must constantly adapt. This can be achieved via changes in price level and in price differentiation according to quality. The information farmers receive via prices depends upon the price determination method used. For example, a deadweight price with grading (as is most used for slaughter pigs) gives more information than a price per head.

When there are a number of submarkets it may be necessary to give the producer compulsory directions in order to obtain a product that is better adapted to market requirements. This can be done by concluding contracts. In the decision to conclude a contract other arguments can also play a role. The main reason for concluding contracts in the calf sector is market risk; in the broiler sector, the existence of submarkets and the efficiency gains from co-ordination of supply in the different stages of the marketing chain are important. In the pig sector, several factors determine whether contracts are or are not concluded. For the agricultural producer they are market risk and financing. Trade and industry are especially concerned about stabilizing a proportion of their supplies and sales, and about ensuring that the pig breed they have developed will be kept pure. The co-ordination via contracts relates largely to quality.

To protect the farmers position "general terms of contract" have been drawn up in consultation with the parties involved and regional advisory committees have been established.

FUTURE DEVELOPMENTS AND POSSIBLE POLICIES

An expected smaller rise in income will result in:

i) a smaller growth market volume and
ii) consumers being more critical in terms of price and quality.

These factors make market research much more necessary, for instance for product differentiation. It also necessitates good grading and standardisation rules, and better co-ordination of supply in the marketing chain. The government can play a role in stimulating these developments in the protection of the position of farmers, especially of those involved in contractual production.

The increase in the scale of production will probably continue. In combination with the smaller growth of demand, this will intensify competition, especially the competition via service, discounts, bonuses and product differentiation. To prevent unfair competition, governments will have to give constant attention to the provision of accurate market information on prices, bonuses, discounts and market prospects etc.

Concentration in the retail trade is also likely to increase. Large retailers have their own market policies. Processing firms will only be able to stay independent and competitive with retailers if they concentrate and orient production towards the market at the earliest possible stages. For co-operatives this means a more market-oriented approach including the exercise of control over the production of their members.

B. RELATION BETWEEN FOOD PROCESSING INDUSTRIES AND FOOD DISTRIBUTION

TRADE RELATIONS BETWEEN FOOD MANUFACTURERS AND DISTRIBUTORS IN FRANCE

by

M. B. Yon
Institut de Gestion Internationale
Agro-alimentaire (IGIA)
France

The purpose of this paper is to furnish an up-to-date review of price formation between manufacturers and distributors and to make suggestions for improving the process in France.

The contract drawn up between a manufacturer and a wholesale food purchaser is the basic element which reveals the relative bargaining strength of the two partners. The transaction determines the allocation of resources between them and hence their likely future economic position. More precisely, the market for manufactured products delivered for sale to consumers is made up of a multitude of bilateral trade negotiations between each manufacturer and each of his customers. It is thus more exact to speak of negotiated trade bargains than of a market. If we wish to know what the terms of those bargains are, we are touching on the very basis of the economic strength of the manufacturing and distributing firms.

Outline of a trade bargain

The elements entering into the bargain are as follows:

- price list and conditions of sale;
- end-of-year rebates;
- business co-operation arrangements;
- supplementary conditions;

- sales promotion arrangements;
- credit and payment terms.

The manufacturer offers the buyer a basic price list representing his official selling prices. From those prices are deducted discounts in respect of:

a) quantity ordered
   - sliding scale
   - quantity discounts
b) services provided by the buyer
   - wholesaling
   - warehousing
   - distribution
c) payment terms
   - discount for cash
d) sales promotion

These discounts are either allowed automatically and uniformly to all purchasers in consequence of their being entered on the manufacturer's list, or are negotiated between the manufacturer and each purchaser individually if they are not included in the former's general conditions of sale.

The discounts listed above are shown on the invoice prepared by supplier, and make up what is known in the French food trade as the "marge avant" (manufacturer's open discount). The purchaser thus knows the basic price of a product as delivered at the point of sale: this is the list price less the various discounts, and it serves as a base for calculating the retail selling price which will be set by adding distribution costs and the distributor's margin.

This basic price is not however the price actually paid by the distributor, as he also receives further rebates which are not shown on the invoice and are paid at the end of the year or at the end of the quarter. These are of two kinds:

- end-of-year rebates related to annual targets (ristournes de fin d'année - RFA);
- rebates related to "business co-operation" between manufacturer and distributor. The rebates, whatever their type and the form in which they are paid (annually or quarterly), do not appear on the seller's invoice. They constitute the "marge arrière" (manufacturers concealed discount).

The distinction between the elements of the "marge avant" and the "marge arrière" is not always clear.

These various notions may be summarised in the following table:

OUTLINE OF PRICE FORMATION BETWEEN MANUFACTURERS AND DISTRIBUTORS

List Price

"Marge Avant"

Manufacturer's general conditions of sale

less

a) Sliding-scale discounts
   Discounts for large quantities

b) Discounts for services

   - Wholesaling
   - Warehousing
   - Retailing

c) Discounts for sales promotion

d) Discounts for cash

Basic Price

"Marge Arrière"

Conditions set by purchaser

less

a) End-of-year rebates (RFA) for:
   - Turnover (organisation or individual member)
   - Volume
   - Increase in turnover or volume

b) Business co-operation rebates for:

   - Range of products
   - Geographical region
   - Back-up sales promotion
   - Trying out and launching new products

True Selling Price

Assessment of the functioning of the price formation system, and proposals

The transparency that is essential to the proper functioning of the market is notoriously inadequate, and the price discovery mechanism for the products is very imperfect in consequence. It follows from this that the selling price for a given product may differ significantly between one manufacturer and another, and between one customer and another of the same manufacturer (by as much as 25 per cent in extreme cases). There is thus no single market price, but a constellation of negotiated prices, the range of which can be attributed to a small extent by economies of scale on sales and delivery, and to a much larger extent by the bargaining power of one or the other partner in the trade negotiation.

These serious imperfections lead to a poor allocation of resources between manufacturers and distributors and thus, in the long run, to an excessive rise in costs leading eventually to a retail price higher than that which would result from a market which achieved an optimum allocation of resources.

Improving the transparency of transactions has been a major cause of concern to the authorities, which explains the requirement they have placed on firms to have a price list and sliding scale available to all those requesting it. The former requirement is complied with in France, but the list price is not yet the actual selling price because of the practice of the "business co-operation contract". It is desirable and feasible that buyers wishing to subscribe to such a contract should be obliged to have it written down, with a scale of application, and to make these two documents available to anyone on request. Such contracts might include scales of rebates for:

- range of products;
- increase in turnover;
- launching of new products;
- advertising back-up.

Anything going beyond these basic provisions should be prohibited.

It would seem that some simple requirements for disclosure, a strict codification of the provisions allowable in business co-operation contracts, and the abolition of delayed payments, should suffice to make a major change in commercial relationships, provided that there is no hidden understanding between the trading partners.

ASPECTS OF A CHANGING RELATIONSHIP BETWEEN FOOD MANUFACTURING AND DISTRIBUTORS IN THE U.K.

by

Mr. J. A. Beaumont

and

Mr. C. Khamis
Institute of Grocery Distribution

Introduction

The issue of the relationship between the food manufacturer and distributor is one which is constantly under debate in the United Kingdom food trade. As this relationship involved the transfer of some £12,000 million worth of goods in 1979, ultimately representing some 15 per cent of consumer spending, it is not surprising that it generates a high degree of interest among both food companies and policy makers.

Much of what has been written about this subject has been restricted to concern about manufacturers' terms to their customers. The purpose of this paper is not to deal with this in detail, but to give an indication of the broader aspects of the relationship and to discuss the more important elements of change.

The chart in the annex situates this relationship in the broader context of the whole food industry. It is with the estimated £11,050 million sold mainly to grocery wholesalers and grocery retailers that we shall primarily be concerned.

BASIC TRADING CHARACTERISTICS IN THE FOOD INDUSTRY

An important influence on trading conditions over the past two decades has been the static nature of the food market which results from virtually constant per capita food spending and population. Such a constraint on total market size conflicts with the search for growth among the main companies. This leaves three basic outlets for company growth: acquisition, diversification and winning food sales from other organisations.

All three have been observed in all sectors of the food trade and this has led to increased concentration at all levels, particularly in retailing.

CONCENTRATION IN THE FOOD INDUSTRY

The relationship between food manufacturers and distributors is now largely a matter of large firms dealing with large firms.

According to estimates by the Institute of Grocery Distribution, 30 food manufacturing firms account for more than 40 per cent of sales of this sector. Of the approximately 250 grocery wholesaling firms operating in 1979, the largest ten accounted for more than 55 per cent of the sales.

In grocery retailing, there has been a concentration in the number and size of both enterprises and outlets. The market share of multiples (companies with ten or more outlets) has risen from an estimated 5 per cent in 1900 to over 55 per cent in 1980 and that of the top 3 firms to over 25 per cent.

Store numbers have fallen by over a half since 1961, but store size has grown. Around 1,000 outlets of over 10,000 sq.ft. selling area account for around 40 per cent of grocery retailers' sales.

SIZE AND BARGAINING POSITION

At the centre of discussions on "bargaining strength" is the declining number of increasingly powerful operators on both sides of the buyer-seller relationship (but particularly amongst buyers) as certain trading benefits may accrue to companies because of their sheer size.

A number of strands in these discussions can be unravelled. First, better terms may arise directly from economies of scale, such as savings in administrative costs and in delivering full, rather than part loads.

Secondly, there are other, real but harder to quantify reasons for more favourable terms such as the benefit to a manufacturer of guaranteed large-scale distribution. However, it is probably true that instances of discrimination do occur in the grocery trade because of manufacturers' fears of the imposition of effective sanctions by large distributors.

Such sanctions range from total withdrawal of the line to varying degrees of shifting emphasis into alternative brands. While the former has occurred, its widespread use is probably limited because of the lack of major brand alternatives in most brand markets. Almost certainly, the true sanction lies in the latter which can be effective as food manufacturing profitability is volume sensitive.

While such market power may seriously harm an individual supplier, for the manufacturing industry as a whole the situation is less serious in the long term as, if supplies are to be ensured, prices cannot be forced below a level which affords the industry an adequate return. However problems may arise if profitability does not allow an adequate investment programme and if research and development funding is impaired. Another possible effect is to encourage the trend to retail concentration.

ADDITIONAL ASPECTS OF THE CHANGING BEHAVIOUR

There are a number of other important areas of change being induced by increasing concentration. First, there is an impact on the role and size of the salesforce. Concentration in the number of enterprises has drawn together into larger blocks certain sales functions such as product listing and price negotiation. Outlet concentration has drawn together the more physical tasks such as stocktaking and merchandising. Both these trends have resulted in the need for fewer, but better trained and more articulate personnel. There has also been a reappraisal of the whole structure of the sales planning function with, for example, an orientation towards major customer accounts rather than brands.

Secondly, changes in physical distribution have been induced by a combination of concentration and rising fuel/distribution costs. Large retailers have exerted a far greater influence on the type and control of distribution facilities, either insisting on manufacturers delivering direct to their stores or direct to the retailer's own depot. Retailers' influence has also been felt on more specific aspects such as the use of cage pallets.

A third change has been in the siting of the main marketing initiative. While in the 1950s and 1960s the emphasis was largely with the food manufacturer with the retailer passively acting as a bridge to the consumer, a manufacturer must now make marketing decisions with a view to likely retailer as well as consumer reaction. This has gone along with competition within retailing leading to the emergence of grocery retailers as "brands" in their own right. Thus retailers' media advertising expenditure rose six-fold between 1970 and 1979. Distributors' own brands, for some retailers, have also played a role here, being positioned in direct competition with the main brands, equal in quality and consumer perception.

Ironically, these trends, which reduce the number of viable large-scale brand alternatives available to retailers, may further increase the level of concentration among food manufacturers.

CHANNELS OF FOOD DISTRIBUTION
£ million (1979)

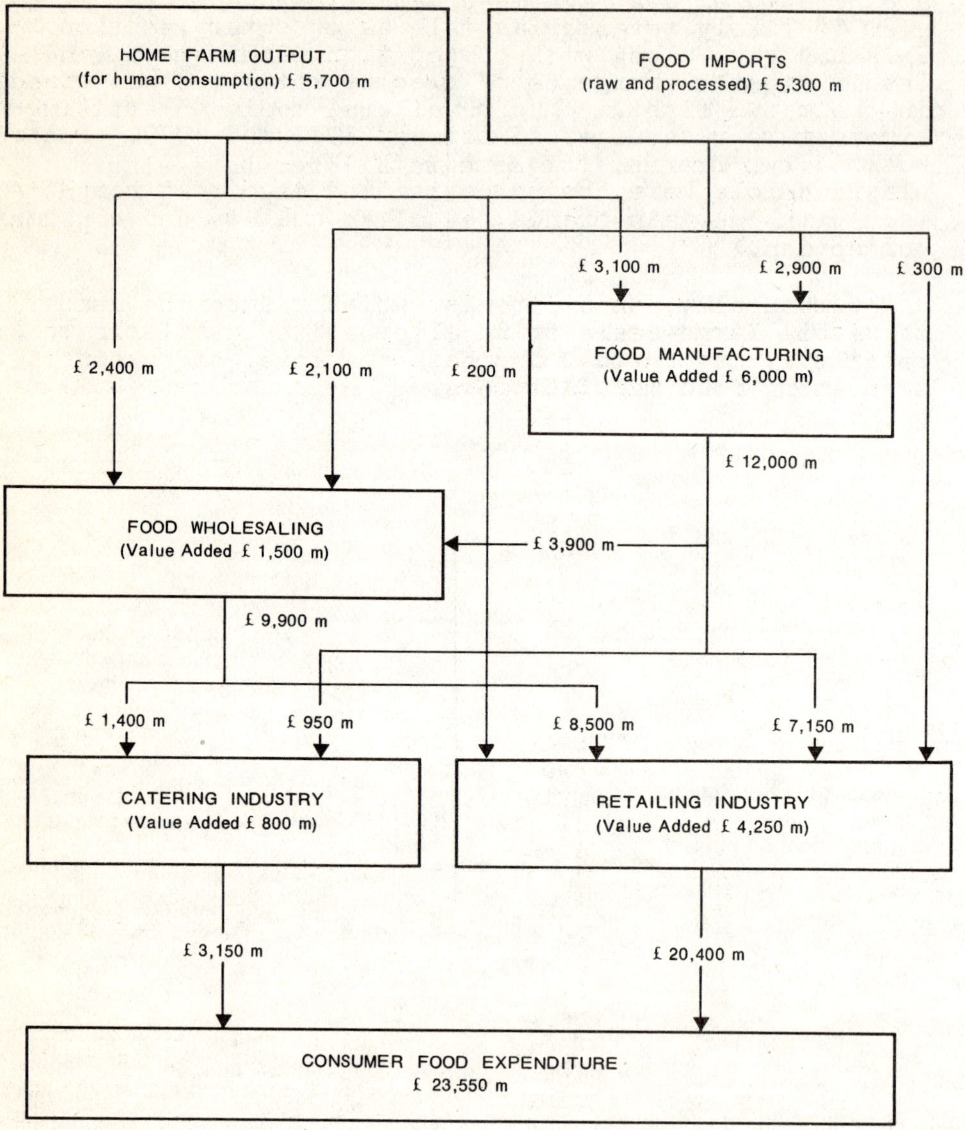

Source : IGD estimates.

RETAILER MANUFACTURER RELATIONSHIPS IN THE FOOD SECTOR (SOME OBSERVATIONS FROM THE USA)

by

Mr. L. G. Hamm
Economic Research Service
United States Department of Agriculture

The basic elements defining the power relationships between buyers and sellers are incorporated with an industrial organisation framework from economics and are presented in Figure 1. Power in the exchange process is primarily a function of: the degree of competition in the industry; the relative importance of the other industry to the sales or purchases of the industry in question; and the potential for one industry to integrate some or all of the functions of the other industry.

The critical aspect of bargaining between buyers and sellers is that the outcomes (conduct and performance) feed back into the basic economic and structural conditions in the buying and selling industries. Consequently, today's bargained outcome can influence the power distribution between buyers and sellers tomorrow. Thus, many of the evolving structural trends in industries logically flow from the interactive relationships of retailers and manufacturers.

The most significant difference between food products sold through food retail outlets is whether they are the retailer's own label products or whether they carry the brand identification of the manufacturer. Brand food products are conceived, usually manufactured, distributed and marketed under the manufacturer's control. Private distributor label products are items whose identity is largely determined by the food retailer. Often retailers do not design or manufacture the product. Rather they purchase the product from a manufacturer who chooses not to or is unable to develop distribution and marketing functions for the product. Since retail food buyers have different degrees of responsibilities for brand versus private label food items, the bargaining

Figure 1,

ELEMENTS OF BUYER-SELLER BARGAINING POWER WITHIN A GENERAL INDUSTRIAL SECTOR FRAMEWORK

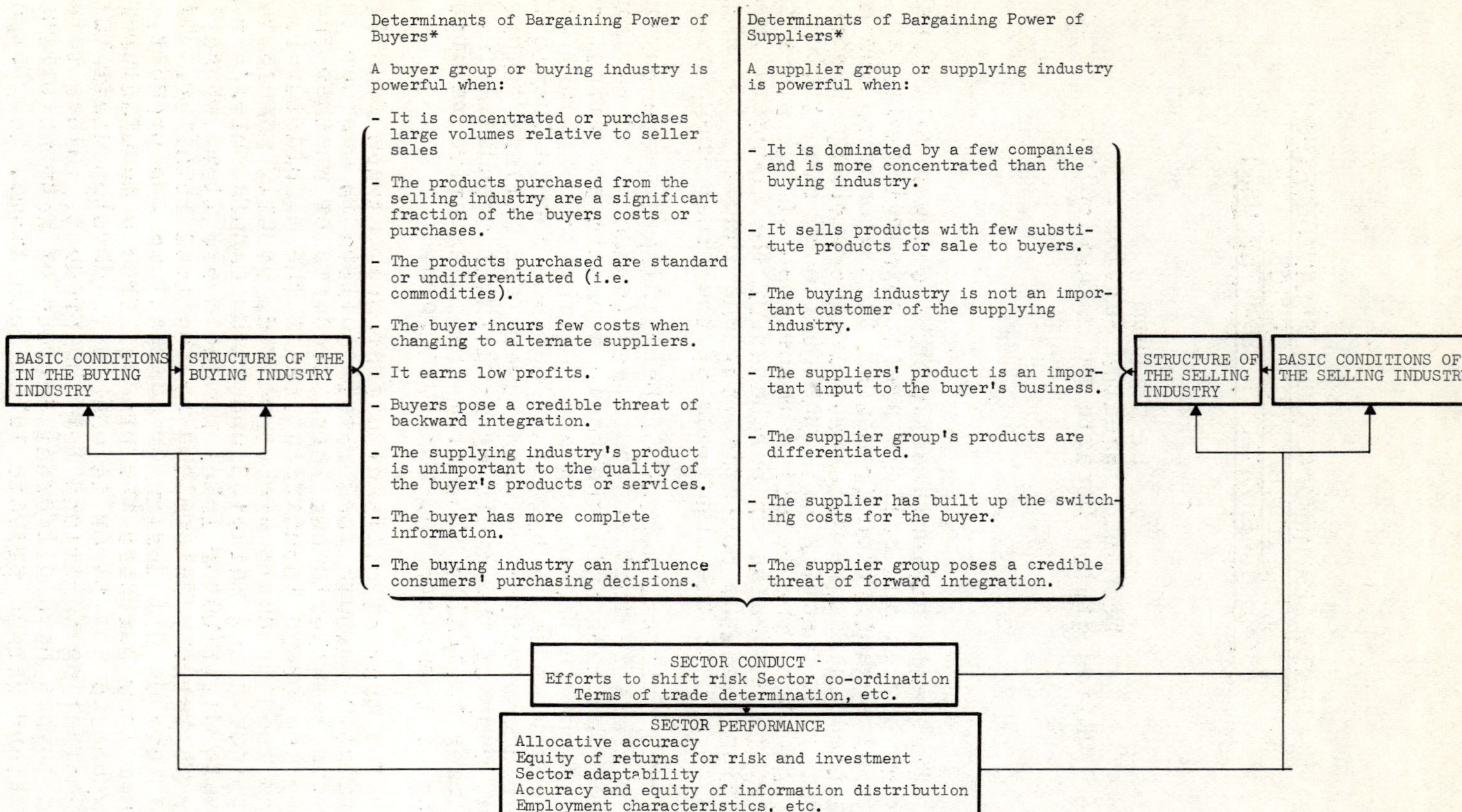

*) This list was adopted from Michael E. Porter Competitive Strategy: Techniques for Analysing Industries and Competitors, The Free Press (New York) Collier MacMillan Publishers (London), 1980, pp. 24-29.

relationships of food retailers with brand food manufacturers and private label processors will be different.

Success for any brand manufacturer is dependent on gaining entry into grocery stores. New product campaigns are given in written form to all grocery buyers in the geographic market where the manufacturer is trying to establish the new item. Manufacturers develop elaborate programmes (called "deals") which contractually link a wholesale price reduction with retailer marketing actions for the manufacturer's product. Table 1 enumerates the provisions and gives an example of fairly standard promotion programmes offered by manufacturers. The essence of retail distributor-food manufacturer bargaining in the United States focuses on the composition of these formal promotion programmes. The retailers would like to have the price reductions with the minimum amount of marketing concessions on their part. Conversely, the manufacturers attempt to maximise retailer marketing activity directed toward their products for a given price reduction.

Within the framework developed in Figure 1, the bargaining power relationship between retailers and brand manufacturers is largely a balance between the degree of retailer control of consumer access and manufacturer's ability to create product differentiation. Since the process of selling brand food products and managing their flow through the distribution system tends to be transferable across product types, conglomerate food marketing tends to be a natural by-product of successful brand marketing. As manufacturers become increasingly large with more differentiated products, retailers must adopt strategies to keep the relative balance of power stable. The most obvious strategy is to grow larger and therefore control more consumer access. A more direct approach is to develop their own products.

Food retailers' interactions with private label suppliers are a marked contrast to those with brand manufacturers. An individual private label manufacturer has no incentive to advertise or promote. Consequently price is more critical in bargaining between private label suppliers and retail buyers. Without differentiated products, private label manufacturers are at the mercy of large private label buyers. These buyers, if they take a short-term view, could force small and medium size manufacturers to sell below cost. In the long term, however, the buyers would create a more concentrated manufacturing industry.

In the United States food sector, the actions of food retailer buyers in their dealings with food manufacturers seem to be dynamically altering the structure of food manufacturing industries. Large brand manufacturers' product differentiation strategies generate

Table 1

GROCERY MANUFACTURER PROMOTION PROGRAMMES

Standard Deal Provisions	Example of a Specific Promotion
1. Local Market Area Covered	To all our customers in the Greater Detroit market area.
2. Product Identification	NB Peanut Butter - 12/18 ounce Smooth Bumpy UPC-72046 UPC-72004
3. Promotion Period - Time period during which price reduction is offered a) First Shipping Date - First day when price product can be shipped to distributor warehouse b) Last Order Date - Last day for accepting buyers orders for deal merchandise c) Last Shipping Date - last day for distributors' orders to be shipped from manufacturer's warehouse	March 31st, 1980 - April 25th, 1980 a) March 31st, 1980 b) April 18th, 1980 c) April 25th, 1980
4. Performance dates - Time period during which retailers must execute the stipulated requirements set down by the manufacturer.	March 31st, 1980 - May 10th, 1980
5. Terms of the Promotion - Stated Reduction off list price; method by which this price reduction is passed on to the distributor; and statement of retailers responsibility.	$1.44 Special Advertising Merchandise Allowance on 18 ounce NB Peanut Butter will be deducted from the invoice or paid by NB Foods, inc. at the end of the performance period on all shipments during the above period providing the retailer qualifies as listed below.
6. Performance Conditions - Standard legally binding performance contracts are written by manufacturers and signed by retailers. Provisions vary according to manufacturers marketing strategies. Some specific classes of provisions include: a) Require a retailer controlled coupon for a specific price reduction to be placed in retailer's advertisements. b) Require the retailer allocate space and/or time in retailer paid advertising to the promoted product at the promotion price. c) Require that the promoted product be given, for a specific time period, different shelf location and/or instore advertising support than that normally given to the product. d) Require that co-operative, affiliated and unaffiliated wholesalers provide their retail accounts with the option to participate in this promotion.	Standard form of performance contract utilised with all accounts. a) Include in regular principle newspaper ads or handbills a 12¢ (minimum value) "throw-away" store coupon. NB Foods is not responsible for any redemption or handling costs. Coupon will be good on 18 oz. NB Peanut Butter (Smooth or Bumpy) at stores noted in advertisement in which a coupon appears. b) Place a two column inch ad in regular principle newspapers for 18 oz. NB Peanut Butter showing 12¢ (minimum) price reduction below regular price during the performance period. c) Display separate and apart from regular shelf space featuring 18 oz. NB Peanut Butter at a 12¢ (minimum) price reduction below regular price for at least one week during the performance period. d) Wholesaler must publish to all accounts (in bulletins or manner usually used) informing accounts that they will pay allowance for a minimum period of three consecutive weeks. Bulletin should state that allowance is payable to retail customers for performing according to terms of the NB Foods, Inc. contract.
7. Stock protection Clauses - Statements that are designed to eliminate the possibility that retail buyers will suffer inventory losses as the result of the manufacturers price reduction.	For all merchandisers accepting this contract, unsold stocks in buyers' warehouses, except Foodservice and Industrial users, shipped between March 3rd, 1980, and March 31st 1980, and not to exceed prior 30 days shipments will be protected to the full amount of promotional allowance, regardless of price at which billed. This applies to off-invoice allowance or to performance promotions when customer signs contract.
8. Terms - Standard Payment Terms	2% for cash in 10 days will be allowed on the gross amount of the invoice before deduction of this allowance, providing remittance is mailed to address designated on invoice
9. Advertising - statement of manufacturer provided advertising support	Heavy prime time network and spot TV on ABC, CBS and NBC during promotion period.
10. Miscellaneous Provisions - statements added which attempt to prevent retailer attempts to subvert the performance contract.	a) NB Foods, Inc. reserves the right to limit quantities purchased by merchandiser. b) Merchandise sold under the terms of this allowance is offered for resale only in the above market area.

profits sufficiently large so that they can continue to grow and prosper. In the private label segment of the United States industry, retailer procurement power forces suppliers to be the lowest cost producers and encourages expansion into other food market segments. Over the long run, retailer bargaining power could diminish as brand and private label suppliers decrease in numbers and increase in relative size.

A price discrimination law probably has some benefits for any food system. Because these laws deal with price systems, they tend to be costly and difficult to administer consistently over time. Whether the benefits outweigh the costs is always debatable. Benefits are most likely to occur when one sector having significant procurement power because of horizontal industrial concentration interfaces with another sector characterised by small firms with little or no ability to differentiate their products. The operation of the Robinson-Patman Act (the United States price discrimination law) has made it largely ineffective in protecting small specialised private label suppliers. However, the United States price discrimination law was written to protect buyers from other buyers and therefore was not originally intended to protect sellers.

As retailers and manufacturers interactions dynamically feed through sector conduct and performance back to basic structural conditions in their industries, new technologies and realigning world economic forces are altering the basic demand and supply conditions in the food sector. These simultaneous flows of influence will reshape the basic bargaining positions of food retailers and food manufacturers.

Several developments in the United States might be significant for retailer power. One is the emergence of a functional Universal Product Code (UPC) computerised laser scanning technology. Another is the increased foreign ownership of United States food retailers. The development of more sophisticated and extensive retailer label strategies can also alter the balance of power. There are other forces at work in the United States food sector helping food manufacturers maintain or gain bargaining power. However, many observers are predicting that United States food retailers will continue to increase their power relative to food manufacturers.

C. ADDITIONAL PAPERS

CONSUMER ORGANISATIONS' VIEW ON EEC FOOD ISSUES

by

Mr. T. Venables
Director of BEUC

BEUC is a European grouping of consumer organisations, the majority of which derive their resources from publication of information to guide consumers' choice through comparative tests and surveys. Our task in Brussels is to represent consumer interests, i.e. through the Commission's various consultative bodies: the Consumers Consultative Committee and specifically in the food sector, the advisory committees for agricultural products, for foodstuffs and for veterinary questions.

An important part of our work is devoted to food issues, partly because of the priority given to the Common Agricultural Policy by the EEC and the fact that this is the only common policy which has an evident impact on consumers. BEUC has campaigned for years for reform of the CAP, which should become a genuine food policy, taking into account not only the interests of farmers, but also of consumers and all other sectors in the food chain. The aim of any food policy should be "to ensure on a continuous basis that sufficient food in terms of quality and quantity is available for consumers at reasonable prices". It must involve more balanced representation of all interests concerned and greater clarity when decisions are taken about their consequences for producers, the food industry and consumers. This is no easy task; it is often difficult even to reconcile the conflicting demands made by consumers themselves, who have different interests depending on their purchasing power. In the current climate of inflation, consumers are becoming more demanding both about food prices and at the same time about health and quality standards. If it is difficult to respond to these apparently contradictory demands in any national food policy, it is all the more difficult in a European or international context because eating habits are quite rightly very different from country to country.

Subject to this reservation and differences of emphasis among consumer organisations which do exist, the following is a common "shopping list" of demands on prices, quality and health standards, at least in relation to EEC policy:

1. Food prices

   If the aim of any food policy is to introduce greater clarity about the impact of decisions then the EEC Commission should also, on the basis of its own Treaty obligations, "to ensure that food reaches consumers at reasonable prices", analyse the impact of the CAP and other costs on food prices. BEUC has been publishing its own analyses of the cost of the CAP both on the EEC budget and on food prices as a way of pointing out that currently there is no satisfactory mechanism for taking consumer interests into account in the common agricultural policy. As long as this is the case, prospects for reform look remote since the narrow budget cost of agricultural policies is not a sufficient mechanism to bring about such a reform.

   Analysis of the effects of CAP support prices on food prices has to take into account the growing share of transformation, packaging, transport costs, middleman's profits and advertising in the price of food. These factors should be examined and the results of price surveys published, not in order to introduce EEC price control but to contribute to improving competition policy and distribution systems. Perhaps the most urgent priority, as far as food prices are concerned, is one which does not relate to the EEC but to the local level: the need to supply regular advice to consumers in a market where prices are subject to excessive local variations.

2. Food safety, health and quality standards

   Before enumerating our demands in relation to EEC food law, it has to be pointed out that the CAP has so far received over-riding priority and is discussed purely outside the context of quality and environmental aspects of agricultural product, and also that historically the EEC has given more priority to animal welfare than to public health standards in food. Nevertheless there are reasons why this could well change. Firstly, the priority consumers themselves are giving to quality standards, and the realisation that the wider market and European competition is often used to argue against stricter legislation or controls. This was underlined by BEUC in the "hormones in veal" affair. Secondly, the recent judgments by the European Court of Justice, reaffirming the principles of the Common Market that products legally produced and sold in any one country can be sold throughout the Community (c.f. "Cassis de Dijon"). This ought to mean that the consumer protection can no longer be seen as just a national issue.

The following are the main issues of concern to consumer organisations:

i) Food safety

BEUC has proposed the setting-up of a "dangerous products interpol" to ensure that all products, including food products, which are found to be unsafe in one country are not exported to the rest of the EEC or dumped on third markets. The tragedy of the Spanish cooking oil affair has highlighted the need for such a system and also showed up the lack of co-ordinated action as governments reacted in different ways to the problem. There is already informal co-operation over dangerous or contaminated foods and health risks associated with them, and we are also circulating such information. The next step should be to make the EEC system more official and to extend it to other parts of the world through international organisations, such as OECD and the UN agencies.

ii) Health and quality standards for food

The EEC Commission has achieved recognition of the principle of "positive lists" in food additives should not be used and included on such lists until their harmlessness has been proved. This, coupled with the setting up of scientific committees is an important step forward. BEUC would like to see the scientific committees strengthened to carry out original research and their own investigations, rather than relying on files submitted by manufacturers and existing scientific literature.

iii) Controls

In the current climate better enforcement of existing laws rather than new legislation is the key issue. There is a need for greater clarity over the costs of enforcing higher health and quality standards. This does not mean subjecting consumer legislation to strict cost-benefit analysis: for example, measures for the prevention of diseases associated with overconsumption and an unbalanced diet, or to eliminate carcinogenic substances should not be assessed in purely financial terms. There is though a tendency to meet all demands from consumers for new legislation or better controls of existing laws, with the objection "it is bound to put up food prices". This may be true in some cases but not in others. We are also sceptical about the argument that the cost of controls should be borne by the producer rather than by public authorities. It is probable that much could be done to improve existing enforcement measures without greatly increasing costs: e.g. better co-operation among different government departments and national agencies responsible for enforcement through all the stages of production and marketing, better European and international co-operation, heavier fines and sanctions as a deterrent to abuse of the law.

iv) Information

Objective information to consumers must come primarily from the organisations which carry out tests and surveys, and they do certainly help to develop a critical awareness of the problems to guide people's choice. But this is also an area for national and European legislation:

- The EEC Member States should ensure as quickly as possible that the food labelling directive is implemented, keeping exemptions to an absolute minimum and avoiding divergent interpretations, e.g. on date-marking. BEUC is currently investigating its implementation and the signs are not encouraging.... It is important though that this directive should succeed to meet both the consumers' interest in having a description of the origin, composition and durability of products whether domestic or foreign, and the manufacturers interest in overcoming barriers to exports.

- The importance of the food labelling directive lies also in the fact that it is a basic framework for follow-up measures in particular.

- Health and other claims in foodstuff labelling and advertising. The Commission's proposals are meeting with some objections from the food industry. On the need for such a measure, there should be little disagreement. False claims cast considerable confusion in a situation where there is growing public concern to have objective information about the nutritional value of food.

- Nutritional labelling, is an obvious next step and a few manufacturers and retailers are introducing it; it is correct in relation to this type of labelling to recognise the dangers of over-complexity. A simplified standard form of information is needed for consumers to be able to compare the nutritional value of different foodstuffs. Consumer organisations often repeat their broad objectives for a "balanced diet" - less fat, sugar, etc, - but what does this mean in practice? Consumers are confused by conflicting claims (e.g. about butter and margarine) and nutritional experts do not agree among themselves. Beyond labelling measures, governments ought to provide, as part of a food policy, more information about national nutritional habits and recommend where changes should be made.

CONCLUDING REMARKS

The concept of a food policy involves wider considerations than those mentioned here, such as the relationship between agricultural policies and general economic objectives and the interests of other countries. For consumer organisations, in relation to the EEC, the general objectives can be defined more narrowly:

- The CAP should be reformed to be seen as part of a food policy and the first need is to ensure better balance of all interests in the food chain and to analyse the effects of decisions on food prices. BEUC is also concerned that greater priority should be given by the EEC to European legislation on health and quality standards for food in particular by strengthening the role of the scientific committees. In the immediate future, priority should be given to establishing a European early warning system to ensure food safety and to the implementation of the food labelling directive, which is important because it should be followed-up by other measures.

Finally, the concept of the food policy means looking at the food sector as a whole and this should result in better co-ordination among the different government departments dealing with food issues.

APPLICATION OF THE COMMUNITY RULES ON COMPETITION TO THE FOOD SECTOR

by

M. J. F. Verstrijnge
Legal Service
Commission for the European Communities
Brussels

The Community rules on competition (Articles 85 to 90 of the EEC Treaty) are directly applicable to the food industry by virtue of the case law of the Court of Justice of the European Communities. The derogations allowed under Council Regulation No. 26/62 for the production and trade in agricultural products do not permit any specific action to be taken which would modulate the application of the European Community's competition policy on the basis of special features of the food industry.

Economic surveys carried out by the Commission of the European Communities in this sector have revealed that a broad balance of power exists between the main groups and that the market structure might be described as a broad and balanced oligopoly, dominated by well-known large firms e.g. Unilever and Nestlé.

Among the many individual cases where infringements under the Community rules on competition have been presented the following cases can be mentioned: FRUBO (collective exclusive rights for the marketing of citrus fruit by auction sales at Rotterdam), EUROPEAN SUGAR INDUSTRY (territorial protection between competitors on the sugar market and economic pressure on dealers), UNITED BRANDS (abuse of dominant position on the banana market), LIEBIG (exclusive purchasing rights intended to exclude competitors from supermarket distribution channels) and RENNET (exclusive purchasing rights by a dominant production co-operative).

Through such measures at both food production and distribution levels, and with the broad support of the Court of Justice, the Commission has acted vigorously to prevent the solidification of anti-competition practices, which had tended to be induced in the markets concerned. The Comission's action has been supplemented by its relatively favourable attitude towards the better organisation of small and medium enterprises in this sector (e.g. purchasing groups, export centres, etc.) with the object of enabling them more easily to face up to competition from the large multinationals.

The application of the rules of competition by the European Community has therefore helped to maintain fluid market structures in the food industry sector. Generally speaking, competitive mechanisms tend to operate normally in the food industry. The action taken by the authority responsible for applying Community Rules on competition is no different from that taken in other sectors. There are however no economic surveys available that could be used for a more detailed analysis of the application of the rules of competition in this sector.

THE IMPACT OF THE COMMON AGRICULTURAL POLICY ON FOOD PROCESSING FIRMS(1)

by

H. E. Buchholz and E. Schmidt, Braunschweig
Institute of Agricultural Market Research
Federal Research Center for Agriculture(1)
Braunschweig-Volkenrode
Germany

The price and market regulations of the CAP have direct effects on all buying and selling activities of food processing and manufacturing firms. Other management activities of such enterprises e.g. production policy, cost minimisation, investment strategies and financial decisions are influenced indirectly. In discussing the direct consequences, reference is made to the situation of particular processing industries in the Federal Republic of Germany. The examples are the milling industry, starch factories, dairies and sugar plants.

The effects of administrative price and market regulation on the buying and selling activities of enterprises in the food processing industries narrow down the scope for individual decision making and thus enhance the dependence from political action which is not necessarily motivated by economic reason. Uncertainty about sudden and severe changes is greatly increased, although uncertainty with respect to price and quantity levels is reduced.

Such consequences are the more important for the industry as in the particular marketing situation of food processing firms the scope for further acquisition seems to be quite limited. The uniform image of many food products, and the small market shares of individual suppliers make efficient use of advertising difficult at the firm level. The potential for product differentiation is viewed to be quite narrow and is restricted by

1. Institut für landwirtschaftliche Marktforschung der Bundesforschungsanstalt für Landwirtschaft Braunschweig-Völkenrode (FAL).

a large number of legal requirements. Introduction of new products is associated with high costs and high risks.

Food processing firms facing such marketing conditions normally are hard put to compensate limitations of marketing activities by making more efficient use of other marketing instruments. Therefore, the disadvantages from administrative interference have to be balanced against the advantages from increased price and margin stabilization and/or price and supply guarantees. These contradicting effects on the market and sales situation have consequences for management decisions in all areas of enterpreneurial policy.

The manifold direct or indirect restrictions on entrepreneurial initiative render active response to market opportunities or threats difficult, or even useless. Passive adjustment to administered conditions seems to become the predominant trend instead of positive entrepreneurial action to exploit new opportunities or to adjust to market challenges. Entrepreneurial policy then increasingly takes on traits of incremental behaviour whose frame of reference is the given prescriptions of public policy and/or their steady extrapolation. Increasing risk aversion takes over the decision-making process. In line with this, management strategies become more concerned with internal rationalisation than with market expansion. A symptomatic indication of this tendency is the fact that the top management in food industry enterprises has risen mostly from production departments and not from commercial departments. Another consequence is a widespread tendency to reduce the scope of the firms own entrepreneurial activity and instead to rely on the collective action of business associations (lobbies). Such developments are probably a logical reaction by industry to the agricultural policy trends to which the firms are exposed. Such reaction justifies or even necessitates further administrative incursion into fields which were formerly in the domain of industrial activity e.g. structural adjustment, sales promotion and research and development.

III. PERSPECTIVES OF THE FOOD INDUSTRIES AND RELATED GOVERNMENT POLICIES IN THE 1980s

FUTURE CONSTRAINTS TO THE FOOD INDUSTRIES ARISING FROM POLICY DEVELOPMENTS IN THE ANIMAL PRODUCTION SECTOR IN EUROPE

by

Mr. C. Mackel
Economics Division
School of Agriculture
Aberdeen, United Kingdom

and

Mr. G. van Dijk
Agricultural University of Wageningen
The Netherlands

INTRODUCTION

The vulnerability of the food processing sector to changes in government agricultural policy is increasing because of the higher capital funding required and the longer time horizon for investments. As a result the dependence on raw material supplies has - by implication of the first two aspects - increased.

In all OECD countries there is an increased level of food processing with accompanying capital investment because:

i) Consumers demand a higher level of convenience.
ii) Development of high volume self-service outlets.
iii) Rationalisation of the wholesaling and distribution sector with an increased demand for processing of meat at the slaughter stage.
iv) Automation of plant and machinery.
v) Increasingly stringent health regulations.

Naturally these trends imply the need for careful project evaluation prior to initiation and a lengthening of the period between inception and inauguration of any project. Once on stream the long-term profitability of the plant will be very dependent upon:

i) Availability of sufficient raw material to ensure optimum throughput.
ii) Exact specification of raw material quality.
iii) The price stability of raw materials.
iv) Ready access to anticipated markets both for raw materials and output.

POLICIES AFFECTING RAW MATERIAL AVAILABILITY

Agricultural policy affects the food sector by altering both total supplies and seasonal variation. Changes in the enterprise balance within the agricultural industry, e.g. favouring arable crops at the expense of livestock products, reduces the supply of slaughter animals for the processing industry. Alternatively store livestock producers may be discriminated against, therefore supplies of store livestock dry up, or store producers move their animals to an alternative and more lucrative market. A change in the type of product without a change in enterprise may also be stimulated by policy measures. Often general policy measures are applied ineffectively. For example, under the CAP, price support to beef producers was linked to specific categories of slaughter animals. Therefore, in the Netherlands, because of insufficient attention to commercial practices by the policy makers, this has led to an increased production of bull beef. Much of this bull beef is produced solely for intervention.

A change in the import/export regulations, usually upon health grounds, can have far reaching effects for both importers and exporters e.g. recent Dutch regulations on hormone implants and the United Kingdom's attempt to stop poultry imports via a health ban. The ban is aimed at stopping the spread of disease in live birds, but its effects are also felt at the processing plant level.

Whilst total supply may remain the same, the seasonal availability of supplies may be altered. This type of change can have profound effects on profitability since most modern plants depend upon maintaining optimum throughput all year round. Therefore policies which either shift the seasonality of production or which alter established storage patterns, or which make it very expensive/risky to carry stocks, can have profound effects. Once again the beef regime of the CAP provides an excellent example. Since bull beef is now produced largely for intervention, farmers no longer have to pay attention to seasonal patterns of market demand. Calves are simply produced to suit the preferred calving time of the dairy herd. As a result, marked peaks of oversupply occur which serves to force down market prices at certain periods and direct supplies into intervention. At other times strong market prices fail to attract extra supplies, because of the seasonal bias in the production cycle induced by intervention.

POLICIES AFFECTING RAW MATERIAL COSTS AND MARKET ACCESS

Most government agricultural programmes in OECD countries involve price rather than income support for farmers. Therefore, any attempt to support the income of marginal farms via price leads to serious market imbalance as the producers on more productive units respond to the higher prices. As this level of market imbalance increases government agencies are drawn more deeply into market management. Unfortunately this growing involvement of institutional agencies often leads to further inflexibility and distortions.

Under these conditions processors can face prices which are too high, and they therefore have to seek alternative or substitute supplies. Also the seasonal pattern of prices may change altogether or become, somewhat unexpectedly, more volatile. The whole locus of price formation may shift to a tariff protected internal support system.

Measures of income support to farmers are often implemented by protective action at frontiers. These policy influences may cause great uncertainty e.g. the timing and scale of EEC export subsidies on intervention stocks. The fact that these sales are often backed up by institutionally controlled credit only adds to the uncertainty.

Successful government policy action towards producers should boost confidence and therefore ensure supplies of new materials. However producers may face a great deal of uncertainty because:

- they are not sure if guarantees will continue;
- actual cost increases may not be covered by institutional price increases;
- the operation of the system is too complex to be understood easily;
- delays in the implementations of price increases often occur;
- changes in relative prices between enterprises may occur.

Policies to achieve structural change in agriculture may also lead to uncertainty in the processing sector e.g. the various EEC dairy cow slaughter schemes. These examples make clear that long-term investment plans in dairies and meat plants are often affected by policy changes stirred-up by short-term political expediency.

Quality and health regulation is an issue which is of growing concern to governments. In the Netherlands, the Meat Inspection Act dating from 1922 prescribed that meat, transported to a municipality other than the one in which the meat was first inspected, should be inspected once again. This inspection constraint caused misallocation of capital investment since it shielded some processor groups from competition and kept inefficient municipal slaughterhouses in operation. After its abolition there was an unfortunate over-reaction, with a great deal of new private investment leading to over-capacity.

In the animal production sector the dairy and meat markets are strongly government controlled. Where control mechanisms have intervention as the buyer of last resort then access to consumers is no longer a necessity. There are clear examples in various EEC countries that groups of firms formulate agreements to the effect that one or more firms per group sell for intervention on behalf of the group. In the Netherlands firms exist which procure beef carcasses prepared solely for intervention requirements. These firms may even operate without a normal sales department.

Within the EEC, the agrimonetary system (though created principally to preserve the integrity of the farm price support mechanism) has had profound effects upon the food processing sector. For example, in Great Britain meat plants were placed under considerable economic pressure in the late 1970s as a result of disparities arising out of the MCA system.

These pressures may be attributed to:

i) The unfavourable change in the profitability of livestock relative to cereals.
ii) Supplies of Irish Store Cattle were reduced as these animals were fattened at home.
iii) United Kingdom calves were exported to the continent because of their favourable treatment under the MCA system.

These problems were further accentuated by the fact that many of the firms were undercapitalised or, at the other extreme, had invested heavily in plants to full EEC standards. This latter group had made their investment on the twin assumptions of an expanding European market and the ready availability of animals. They in fact found their margins squeezed as they fought for both market share and throughput.

CONCLUDING REMARKS

In the past firms processing animal products have been influenced by various policy measures applied at the farm level. These effects have been discussed under a few broad headings. In practice the situation is far more complex and it is difficult to disentangle the often conflicting effects of different policy objectives. For example grant aid may be provided to improve both the structure and the productivity of the beef sector, only for monetary policy to make the full implementation of these plans highly unlikely.

Competitive performance is directly affected when market policies stimulate agreements between processing firms as to how to exploit intervention to maximum advantage. This reliance upon support buying reduces the need to actively pursue market research and development.

The most important future constraints for the animal product processing industries seem to be:

i) Government regulations affecting husbandry practices. Such controls, which usually result from public concern over animal health and welfare, can have considerable knock-on effects as they tend to be concentrated in those areas most highly geared to the requirements of the modern food processing sector e.g. poultry and other intensive livestock.

ii) Research and Development.
Responsibility for research and development in animal production at the farm level is likely to shift more to the private sector.

iii) Reallocation of Resources.
Despite its declared aims the effects of EEC agricultural policy has been to distort patterns of regional specialisation. The favourable treatment given to cereals has meant that large areas best suited to grass production have been ploughed up for grain production e.g. Eire and North East Scotland. This development has caused severe supply problems for processing plants located in these traditional livestock rearing areas.

iv) Contractual Arrangements.
One way of improving the optimisation of plant capacity, and ensuring that raw materials suit the exact requirements of the processor, is the increased use of contracts. These contracts could be used to link all sections of the industry from retail to primary producer.

The two key problem areas in this development are:

a) Differences in market knowledge and power between sectors.
b) Agreeing on an equitable price finding mechanism without the normal "free" market mechanisms.

In conclusion, it seems that the complex balance between consumer wants, public concern over animal health and welfare, technological advance in the processing sector, regional variations in animal production and variations in the desired role of agriculture can only be achieved by an integrated policy approach. To pursue an agricultural policy alone is no longer sufficient. A common framework must be found which can take account of agricultural problems, industrial developments and consumer requirements. Only in this framework can all sectors of the industry achieve a satisfactory level of performance.

DEVELOPMENT OF THE FOOD SYSTEM IN JAPAN IN THE 1980s(1)

by

Mr. Y. Ono
Japanese Delegation to OECD

THE ROLE AND PROSPECTS OF THE FOOD INDUSTRY

The food industry(2) has come to occupy an important position in food supply and national economy as a result of the increasing percentage of expenditure for processed foods and for eating out(3) associated with the diversification of dietary habits, and the growth in shipments and sales(4).

In response to the increasingly diverse dietary preferences of consumers due in part to increased job opportunities for women and an increase in number of "nuclear" families, there will be an increase in the supply of foods requiring a higher degree of processing, the rise of attention to quality control and the diversification of food distribution channels.

---

1. Based on the deliberations and recommendations in the report entitled: "Basic Direction of Agricultural Policy in the 1980s", submitted by the Agricultural Policy Council.
2. Food industry consists of food processing industry, food distribution and food service (restaurant) industry.
3. The share of consumer expenditure on food accruing to the distribution, processing and restaurant service sectors increased from 52.8 per cent in 1960 to 63.0 per cent in 1975.
4. The total shipments of the food processing industry reached Yen 20.632 billion, which was approximately 1.4 times larger than agriculture, forestry and fishery production valued at Yen 14.159 billion in 1979.

In the light of increased competition within the food industry, entrepreneurs will be required to make management more efficient and to develop and sell more imaginative merchandise, higher in added-value and better adapted to prevailing consumer preferences.

BASIC DIRECTION OF POLICY

It is important to clarify the position of the food industry within the national economy, to identify the role and inter-relationships among the various sub-sectors, and to define future prospects and guidelines concerning industry activity and business management.

In terms of specific policies for the food industry, a respect for the market principle and for fair competition are fundamental. However, taking into consideration the slower growth of food consumption expenditure and the limited availability of energy resources, losses to the economy resulting from excessive competition should be minimised.

Policies aimed at establishing both fair competition and an efficient distribution and production system, should reflect both the need to give attention to anti-monopoly policy and the need to prevent excessive competition.

DIRECTION OF INDIVIDUAL POLICIES

The basic directions for technology, distribution and the food service (restaurant) industry are as follows:

Technology

- To establish a closer relationship between government, industrial and academic circles.
- To develop a system whereby technical information may be collected, accumulated and utilised.

Distribution

- To lower distribution costs as a whole, placing particular emphasis on specialisation and on the organisation of co-operative and joint-venture type enterprises.
- To encourage a smooth adaptation to environment changes, such as intensification of competition.

- To make transportation and distribution more energy-efficient and to expedite technological developments in the distribution system, in particular in relation to storage, packaging and material handling.
- To reorganise and develop principal and secondary wholesale markets for fresh and perishable foods.

The food service (restaurant) industry(5)

- To encourage technical innovation and to improve management standards.
- To accord particular priority to the food service industry in the context of overall food policy.

5. This industy has yet to mature in terms of management, manpower and organisation because it has thus far progressed too rapidly.

PUBLIC POLICY AND ECONOMIC POWER: THE AMERICAN ANTITRUST LAWS AND SOME INTERNATIONAL COMPARISONS

by

Mr. W.F. Mueller(1)
Food System Research Group
University of Wisconsin
Madison, U.S.A.

The market structure of many American food manufacturing and distributing industries confers substantial market power on the leading corporations in these industries. This power has grown in recent decades and promises to grow further in the future. In this respect the food industries differ little from many other United States industries. Indeed, it is generally acknowledged that in modern capitalistic economies a few hundred corporations have been granted, implicitly if not explicitly, the responsibility for running many important sectors of the economy.

The economic power held by these relatively few corporations often translates into great discretion in corporate economic, social and political policy. Most visibly, it is reflected in the ability to set prices and determine the character and quality of products as well as the expansion and location of manufacturing plants. The choices made on these matters, as well as direct involvement in decisions affecting the arts or the political system, testify to the influence corporations exercise in a nation's social and political character.

In these and other ways the large corporation can set the pattern for the socio-economic-political fabric of our entire system. This is tremendous power and inevitably raises questions concerning the legitimacy of the large corporations' custodianship of particular economic sectors. Contributing to this concern with

---

1. William F. Vilas Research Professor of Agricultural Economics, Professor of Economics, and Professor in the Law School, University of Wisconsin, Madison, Wisconsin, U.S.A.

corporate power are the economic costs such power entails. Studies demonstrate that the corporate custodians of the food manufacturing and distributing industries often possess market power sufficient to impose huge monopoly overcharges on consumers.

The presence of actual or potential corporate power is not new. Democratic societies have long recognised the potential conflict between private corporate interests and the public interest. In the United States, concern with this conflict has waxed and waned over the past century as the nation has experimented with alternative means of social control of private power. The pendulum has swung between the extremes of laissez faire and direct public ownership and/or extensive regulation of business practices. The result has been a mixed economy that, for the most part, is run by private enterprises operating within a rather complex system of public constraints.

In the United States and Europe, there is much to be learned from a comparison of the respective merger laws and enforcement procedures. Students of American merger law should especially examine the public interest defenses commonly found in European law. American antitrust proponents often are intolerant of such defenses, arguing that competition is the only appropriate standard. This is nonsense. Matters relating to a merger's impact on communities, employment, and trade may well transcend in importance the purely competitive effects of a merger. It would be well that American antitrust experts learn from European experience more about the procedures used in weighing these matters. Such defenses would become particularly relevant if legislation were enacted declaring certain types of large conglomerate mergers presumptively illegal.

Insofar as European food corporations have market power they probably have somewhat less to fear from the antitrust laws than do their United States counterparts. Although the United States antitrust laws appear tougher than the European laws surveyed, the effect of this difference on performance may not be all that great for two reasons. First, the United States laws have not been an unqualified success, particularly in the food manufacturing industries. Second, the various European nations may have developed superior alternative methods of social control of private economic power such as consumer co-operatives, price controls, and other government regulations.

Annex 1

THE FOOD INDUSTRIES IN THE INTERNATIONAL STANDARD INDUSTRIAL CLASSIFICATION(1)

31 Manufacturers of Food, Beverages and Tobacco

311. 312 Food Manufacturing

- 3111 Slaughtering, preparing and preserving meat
- 3112 Manufacture of dairy products
- 3113 Canning and preserving of fruit and vegetables
- 3114 Canning, preserving and processing of fish, crustacea and similar foods
- 3115 Manufacture of vegetable and animal oils and fats
- 3116 Grain mill products
- 3117 Manufacture of bakery products
- 3118 Sugar factories and refineries
- 3119 Manufacture of cocoa chocolate and sugar confectionary
- 3121 Manufacture of food products not elsewhere classified
- 3122 Manufacture of prepared animal feeds

313 Beverage Industries

- 3131 Distilling rectifying and blending spirits
- 3132 Wine Industries
- 3133 Malt liquors and malt
- 3134 Soft drinks and carbonated water industries

314 3140 Tobacco manufacturer

---

1. Statistical Papers of the United Nations. Series 19 N°4. Rev. 2, 1968.

OECD SALES AGENTS
DÉPOSITAIRES DES PUBLICATIONS DE L'OCDE

ARGENTINA – ARGENTINE
Carlos Hirsch S.R.L., Florida 165, 4° Piso (Galería Guemes)
1333 BUENOS AIRES, Tel. 33.1787.2391 y 30.7122

AUSTRALIA – AUSTR
Australia and New Zea
10 Aquatic Drive, Frenc
P.O. Box 459, BROOK

AUSTRIA – AUTRICH
OECD Publications and
4 Simrockstrasse 5300
Local Agent/Agent loca
Gerold and Co., Graben

BELGIUM – BELGIQU
CCLS – LCLS
19, rue Plantin, 1070 B

BRAZIL – BRÉSIL
Mestre Jou S.A., Rua C
Caixa Postal 24090, 05
Rua Senador Dantas 19
Tel. 232.07.32

CANADA
Renouf Publishing Com
2182 ouest, rue Ste-Cat
MONTRÉAL, Qué. H3
OTTAWA, Ont. K1P 5

DENMARK – DANEM
Munksgaard Export and
35, Nørre Søgade
DK 1370 KØBENHAV

FINLAND – FINLAND
Akateeminen Kirjakaup
Keskuskatu 1, 00100 H

FRANCE
Bureau des Publications
2 rue André-Pascal, 757
Principal correspondant
13602 AIX-EN-PROVI
Tel. 26.18.08

GERMANY – ALLEM
OECD Publications and
4 Simrockstrasse 5300

GREECE – GRÈCE
Librairie Kauffmann, 2
ATHÈNES 132. Tel. 3

HONG-KONG
Government Informatio
Publications/Sales Secti
2/F., 22 Ice House Stre

ICELAND – ISLANDE
Snaebjörn Jönsson and
Hafnarstraeti 4 and 9,
Tel. 13133/14281/1193

INDIA – INDE
Oxford Book and Statio
NEW DELHI-1, Scindi
CALCUTTA 700016, 1

INDONESIA – INDON
PDIN-LIPI, P.O. Box 3

IRELAND – IRLANDE
TDC Publishers – Library Suppliers
12 North Frederick Street, DUBLIN 1 Tel. 744835-749677

ITALY – ITALIE
Libreria Commissionaria Sansoni :
Via Lamarmora 45, 50121 FIRENZE. Tel. 579751/584468
Via Bartolini 29, 20155 MILANO. Tel. 365083
Sub-depositari :
Ugo Tassi
Via A. Farnese 28, 00192 ROMA. Tel. 310590
Editrice e Libreria Herder,
Piazza Montecitorio 120, 00186 ROMA. Tel. 6794628
Costantino Ercolano, Via Generale Orsini 46, 80132 NAPOLI. Tel. 405210
Libreria Hoepli, Via Hoepli 5, 20121 MILANO. Tel. 865446
Libreria Scientifica, Dott. Lucio de Biasio "Aeiou"
Via Meravigli 16, 20123 MILANO Tel. 807679
Libreria Zanichelli
Piazza Galvani 1/A, 40124 Bologna Tel. 237389
Libreria Lattes, Via Garibaldi 3, 10122 TORINO. Tel. 519274
La diffusione delle edizioni OCSE è inoltre assicurata dalle migliori librerie nelle città più importanti.

JAPAN – JAPON
OECD Publications and Information Center,
Landic Akasaka Bldg., 2-3-4 Akasaka,
Minato-ku, TOKYO 107 Tel. 586.2016

KOREA – CORÉE
Pan Korea Book Corporation,
P.O. Box n° 101 Kwangwhamun, SÉOUL. Tel. 72.7369

LEBANON – LIBAN
Documenta Scientifica/Redico,
Edison Building, Bliss Street, P.O. Box 5641, BEIRUT.
Tel. 354429 – 344425

MALAYSIA – MALAISIE
University of Malaya Co-operative Bookshop Ltd.
P.O. Box 1127, Jalan Pantai Baru
KUALA LUMPUR. Tel. 51425, 54058, 54361

11

eet,

l Office),

2.60

, LAHORE 3.

ILA.

75.46.55
LONA 7.

.45

1. Tel. 022.31.89.50

TAIWAN – FORMOSE
Good Faith Worldwide Int'l Co., Ltd.
9th floor, No. 118, Sec. 2,
Chung Hsiao E. Road
TAIPEI. Tel. 391.7396/391.7397

THAILAND – THAILANDE
Suksit Siam Co., Ltd., 1715 Rama IV Rd,
Samyan, BANGKOK 5. Tel. 2511630

TURKEY – TURQUIE
Kültur Yayinlari Is-Türk Ltd. Sti.
Atatürk Bulvari No : 77/B
KIZILAY/ANKARA. Tel. 17 02 66
Dolmabahce Cad. No : 29
BESIKTAS/ISTANBUL. Tel. 60 71 88

UNITED KINGDOM – ROYAUME-UNI
H.M. Stationery Office, P.O.B. 276,
LONDON SW8 5DT. Tel. (01) 622.3316, or
49 High Holborn, LONDON WC1V 6 HB (personal callers)
Branches at: EDINBURGH, BIRMINGHAM, BRISTOL, MANCHESTER, BELFAST.

UNITED STATES OF AMERICA – ÉTATS-UNIS
OECD Publications and Information Center, Suite 1207,
1750 Pennsylvania Ave., N.W. WASHINGTON, D.C.20006 – 4582
Tel. (202) 724.1857

VENEZUELA
Libreria del Este, Avda. F. Miranda 52, Edificio Galipan,
CARACAS 106. Tel. 32.23.01/33.26.04/31.58.38

YUGOSLAVIA – YOUGOSLAVIE
Jugoslovenska Knjiga, Terazije 27, P.O.B. 36, BEOGRAD.
Tel. 621.992

Les commandes provenant de pays où l'OCDE n'a pas encore désigné de dépositaire peuvent être adressées à :
OCDE, Bureau des Publications, 2, rue André-Pascal, 75775 PARIS CEDEX 16.

Orders and inquiries from countries where sales agents have not yet been appointed may be sent to:
OECD, Publications Office, 2, rue André-Pascal, 75775 PARIS CEDEX 16.

66899-10-1983

OECD PUBLICATIONS, 2, rue André-Pascal, 75775 PARIS CEDEX 16 - No. 42647 1983
PRINTED IN FRANCE
(51 83 08 1) ISBN 92-64-12509-4